About the Author

Nicola Baird is a city-based environmental journalist and mum of two young children. She's also the author of six books, including the co-authored *Save Cash and Save the Planet* (Collins, 2005). She blogs often about fun ways to travel with kids (all without leaving the UK), see www.aroundbritainnoplane.blogspot.com, and also more about baby and childcare at www.homemadekids.co.uk. For surprising insights into eco lifestyles, read the romantic comedy, *There's a Hippo in My Cistern,* written by her football-obsessed husband Pete May (Collins, 2007).

Homemade Kids

Thrifty, Creative
and Eco-Friendly Ways
to Raise Your Child

Nicola Baird

Vermilion
LONDON

1 3 5 7 9 10 8 6 4 2

Published in 2010 by Vermilion, an imprint of Ebury Publishing

Ebury Publishing is a Random House Group company

The Random House Group Limited Reg. No. 954009

Addresses for companies within the Random House Group can be found at www.rbooks.co.uk

A CIP catalogue record for this book is available from the British Library

The Random House Group Limited supports The Forest Stewardship Council (FSC), the leading international forest certification organisation. All our titles that are printed on Greenpeace approved FSC certified paper carry the FSC logo. Our paper procurement policy can be found at www.rbooks.co.uk/environment

Mixed Sources

Product group from well-managed forests and other controlled sources
www.fsc.org Cert no. TT-COC-2139
© 1996 Forest Stewardship Council

Printed in the UK by CPI Mackays, Chatham, ME5 8TD

ISBN 9780091929893

Copies are available at special rates for bulk orders. Contact the sales development team on 020 7840 8487 for more information.

To buy books by your favourite authors and register for offers, visit www.rbooks.co.uk

The information in this book has been compiled by way of general guidance in relation to the specific subjects addressed, but is not a substitute and not to be relied on for medical, healthcare, pharmaceutical or other professional advice on specific circumstances and in specific locations. Please consult your GP before changing, stopping or starting any medical treatment. So far as the author is aware the information given is correct and up to date as at March 2010. Practice, laws and regulations all change, and the reader should obtain up to date professional advice on any such issues. The author and publishers disclaim, as far as the law allows, any liability arising directly or indirectly from the use, or misuse, of the information contained in this book.

Special thanks to Pete and our daughters, Lola and Nell, and also to my own mum.

Contents

Acknowledgements

Many thanks to everyone who helped suggest ideas and interviewees, including the book's first champions, Clare Hulton, Miranda West and Cindy Chan. Plus a special thank you for test reading to new mums Anne Coddington, Stacy Kurokwa-Cook and Andrea Lewis. Also thank you to Justine Taylor, Laura McKay, Jane Hutchings, Yin Yan Wu and Cecily Chu and my agent David Luxton.

Introduction
Bringing up Baby Green

Having a baby can be the perfect opportunity to make practical changes that are good for you and that avoid damaging the planet. If we can resist buying everything new, learn to adapt what we've got and enjoy and appreciate the world around us, then there's a good chance that our babies will grow up with real respect for the planet and an understanding that co-operation is a vital – and life-enhancing – life skill. It should not feel worthy: green baby care is hands-on and fun. For some parents the clincher in these financially challenging times might be that many of the suggestions in this book suit those of us watching our spending. Whatever your motivations, here's to enjoying time spent with our homemade kids.

> My advice to pregnant women wanting to be green is don't buy anything (apart from possibly cloth nappies). You get given loads of stuff, and when you're pregnant it's incredibly tempting to get sucked into the consumer guilt-fuelled hell that is motherhood. New babies need hardly anything, and there's plenty of time to find out what you do really need after they are born. I hardly ever used baby baths, changing mats, baby monitors.
> Caroline, 33, with Madeleine, six, and Rudy, four

All babies need is love, food and a safe place to live. That's all they've ever needed. But if you are pregnant the chances are that you've already drawn up a list of the things that you think a baby must have even before the little 'un appears. Bet it's already longer than a newborn tip to toe. There's still a chance to buck this trend, suppose this year's new arrivals – more than 7,000 babies are born in the UK each day – were raised in a home where thrifty green thinking underpinned most decisions, raising our children would be far less damaging for the environment.

Having fewer children is probably the greenest thing any of us can do. But sex and procreation is not just human instinct – it can be a tremendous pleasure too. Watching your children and their friends grow up is a hard-to-beat joy.

I've spoken to all sorts of families who have thought carefully about what they really need to raise a baby in a world that has to adapt to the challenges of peak oil and climate change. Parents have told me they want their children to grow up to be more cooperative, really good at solving problems, a dab hand at skills like cooking and mending, and knowing where to find what's needed without breaking the bank. If you want your kids to have these skills it helps if you are able to do them too.

'Since having a baby I've become more environmentally conscious, just because there is so much potential for waste and I feel guilty about producing lots of extra rubbish.'
Jude, 34, with Oliver, one

Here's a less altruistic motivation for questioning how you raise your child. If you follow the standard 'What I need for my baby' list for the next 21 years, then your child could cost you over £200,000 (that's £9,500 per year, or £800 per month) even without being privately educated. Done mindfully, choosing the greenest option, or the next best, can make your life cheaper as well as less complicated. Creative reuse of items you already have is thrifty, fun and satisfying. Breastfeeding avoids the need for bottles, formula and a sterilising kit. Co-sleeping means you don't have to move house just to make room for your baby…

Raising your child using green principles is good for the planet, but best of all it makes your baby a big part of your life so that your family can enjoy really happy days of simple pleasures – like a Thermos of tea after leaf kicking together at the park, deftly folding reeds into boats or simply using a twig to race across a puddle or stream.

Green childcare is generous and neighbourly. You borrow and you pass things on. Somehow, passing on items seems to give all the users an instant connection, the modern version of an extended family. Sharing items shows you care not just for your planet, it's also clear evidence that you believe every child matters.

Green days CASE STUDY

For me living life in an eco-friendly way is not a new family trick. I've been getting better at it ever since my girls, Lola, ten, and Nell, eight, were born – partly because having children makes you think much more creatively about the future. My husband is adamant that we shouldn't be 'earnest greens', so our meals aren't always organic, we even occasionally eat takeaway pizza and chips. But we do have some green-tinged principles that we try to apply when we spend. For example, we try to buy only things that we think will last well and we want those things to be ethically sourced, or come from the UK. When we buy something we also want to know the story behind it: where it came from, how it was made, whether it was pre-loved.

Lola was born in a big city in a hospital with no pain relief. Next time I tried a homebirth, again with no pain relief. (I'm lucky, and yes it hurt, but I figured drugs slow down birth so much that I'd rather get the baby out and try breastfeeding ASAP). Our family still lives in the same big city. We have no car, although we are members of a car club. Three of us are vegetarian (Nell eats meat as an occasional treat). We have an amateur vegetable plot in our front city garden, and hens in the back. Using grants, we have installed solar thermal panels to heat our water, and using solar PV panels, we are starting to sell some of our home-generated electricity back to the grid through the renewable energy supplier, Good Energy. It's nice to know our home is doing some work whenever the sun shines, or, in the case of solar PV, whenever it's daylight. Pete and I work from home. We don't earn much but we do what we love. We couldn't afford to work like this at first so we used a combination of swapping childcare with other parents, nannies, childminders, community and private nurseries, enabling Pete to freelance and me to work part-time for ten years at the biggest environmental organisation in the world, Friends of the Earth.

This book gives you the advantages all second-time parents have. These are the mums and dads who know what works and can bathe a baby, change a nappy and cut up veg for teething batons. They know which experts they trust and what really wasted their time (baby food jars and stair gates for me; worrying about sleep training for others). They are the ones who have draught-proofed their home – making it more comfy when the baby is playing on the sitting-room floor as well as less expensive to heat. These families look out for second-hand clothing and are willing to pass on equipment and outgrown clothing to a younger child, whether friend or stranger. They buy from eBay or use Freecycle, or go to a trusted supplier for quality, fair-traded, or certified products (organic, FSC-certified timber, eco-efficient, etc.).

The best bit is that these families are certain that green childcare helps them to raise happy children. Green parents are skilled at getting their children to join in. They manage this by encouraging even the littlest children to do things like feeding themselves or tidying their toys.

Involve your kids as much as you can, from as young an age as you dare, so their participation becomes an integral part of family life. You may need to learn with them – and that will be less of a chore if you try to enjoy the journey. The only drawback to bringing up babies green is that when your children are adults they'll curse you for the lack of misery tales to tell their analyst.

Life-Enhancing Skills

'Now that Finn is older we're realising there's a lot more to green parenting than being a green consumer. We've started to introduce him to the idea of recycling and composting and even at the tender age of two and a half he is doing his bit. We've also planted out seeds with him and put him "in charge" of watering, which he takes very seriously. We're not trying to educate him on any big ideas as such, but simply to start to see the connections between what we do.'

Elaine, 44, with Finn, two, and Niall, two weeks

Parents have always tried to raise their children with an eye to the future – they've passed on silver teaspoons and family heirlooms. They've planted woodlands and left legacies. And they've thrown all they can at education, seeing it as the way to give their child an advantage over their peers. But climate change will have a big impact on the way we need to raise children. We need to find ways to bring them up so they are able to cope with adaptation and learn to be more cooperative.

Our children will also need to be resourceful enough to be more self-sufficient. As parents we set up our children's generation, not just by trying to tackle climate change in the ways that we feel able to do right now, but also by giving our progeny the love and practical skills to handle life in what looks set to be a world where make do, mend and the ability to get on with others will be necessary and life-enhancing.

Childcare matters

> Having a baby makes you rethink your priorities. I've always been really interested in holistic approaches but since the birth of my son, health, happiness and well-being have become top of my list. So much so that I'm retraining to become a homeopath. I'm hoping to practise professionally one day but being able to use what I learn at home on my own family is also really exciting.
>
> Jo, 34, with Billy, 17 months

Breastfeeding your child may be popular with 30-something mums but statistics show that few women exclusively breastfeed until their child is six months, or even continue much after that. If you've had to give up – because you were going back to work, or preferred using formula – aim to be kind to the ones who haven't, rather than treating it as a mum-versus-mum war. And in turn women who are able to raise their children in a very green manner should be kind to you. The media would have you believe that mothers fall into one of three tribes – the workers, the part-timers and the full-timers – all constantly waging battle against one another. This portrayal of mothers is a huge handicap to each of our individual attempts to bring up our babies well. There would be less conflict if we all accepted that everyone is trying to raise their children in the best way that we can.

Although plenty of dads look after their kids throughout the day, most baby and toddler groups are dominated by adult women. Lots of dads at these sessions moan that they only ever get introduced to the other dads, when getting to know a few more mums would have made the experience a bit more interesting. In a greener world we'd perhaps have a better gender balance. Until then, it makes sense to be open-minded about who is holding the baby.

Simple steps to an eco-aware home

Being a greener parent is a way of future proofing climate-change babes one washable nappy at a time. Be proud of yourself for making a start, however small. Here are some ideas to make it simpler:

1. Make less waste

Make less waste is the same principle readers of women's fashion magazines know as 'cost per wear' for what would otherwise be a pricey outfit. The equivalent green mantra is reduce, reuse, refuse, repair, recycle. For example, a **disposable nappy** can only be used once, sometimes for less than an hour, before it has to be thrown away. It may then clog up a landfill site for 400 years or more before it rots down into component parts. In contrast, **washable nappies** can be used many times, over many years. When they are outgrown they can be saved for a future child or passed on to a friend. When they are too tatty to wear the material can be recycled. Using a nappy service is even better because you borrow the nappies, outsource the washing duties and support a useful local business.

Tip

Can you adapt something you already have (or maybe even borrow it)?

Have confidence in your ability to make do, create and mend things – or find someone who can. For instance, you can nibble off your baby's sharp nails with your teeth – far easier than scissors. You can use teaspoons rather than plastic, heat-sensitive spoons when you start giving your baby food from six months. Try making a mobile (from hangers and painted matchboxes, driftwood and shells) to put over your baby's sleeping area. Cereal boxes and toilet roll middles can be transformed into a castle with your toddler. Or turn an outgrown or broken buggy into a go-kart, or revamp an unused sandpit into a sunken garden wetland so it becomes a perfect eco-habitat and, with supervision, a safe place for a toddler to explore for mini beasts. An old door secured on to a low trestle (or even logs) will make a good table for outside eating or messy play. Nothing beats a good book for calm, cuddly entertainment that the littlest child will enjoy again and again. You can make reading even more thrilling for a little child if you use their name instead of the main character's.

2. Learn with your baby

There are some traditionally mumsy skills like knitting and fairy cake decoration which you may already know or learn as your baby grows. But there are so many other things to share with children which we can learn from neighbours, enthusiasts and from experts which, once mastered, will improve your quality of life and may enrich your neighbourhood too.

Newborns are a magnet for know-it-alls who will be adamant about what you should be doing to raise your child properly. You don't have to follow their unsolicited tips, but don't rule out the likelihood that good advice can help you find creative solutions to some unexpected baby conundrums. For example, an older neighbour passed on the useful tip that 'in her day' socks could double up as gloves for a baby's tiny hands so you don't need to make time to go to the charity shop to replace lost gloves.

If you are on maternity leave your baby's first few months may be the first time you've had the chance to get to know your neighbourhood properly. You can have happy days walking in parks, or going to the library after a scan of the community noticeboard to find out what's going on at the weekend. Walking the local pavements is a brilliant way of getting to know the people who live or work nearby.

'Being a parent has made me 100 times more connected with the local community. I know so many local people through play groups, school, being a school governor, attending childminder training and just because I have the time to talk to neighbours. And I mean people from different social backgrounds, with different religions, different cultural backgrounds, and who are much older than me – the workplace offers very little scope for meeting other people. I love this ongoing learning process.'
Jo, 39, with Ben, five, and Sally, two

It's worth remembering that just because an organisation doesn't focus on children doesn't mean that it isn't working hard to change laws to make life better for us all. If you are finding baby care (or the mix of baby care and a job) hard work, then try to support organisations that are helping make your community better. See suggestions in the Resources section.

3. Share the work

'I love getting out of the house so often meet up with friends for a walk at the local arboretum or in the park. There are loads of drop-in baby and kiddy groups where I live – they have tea and toys – so it's very easy. If I am meeting friends at my home we have fair-trade tea and the kids just play. We've stacks of toys from car boot sales over the years and the garden is one big play adventure with a climbing frame from Freecycle and a wooden play house from eBay. '
Zoe, 39, with Mati, six, and Pip, three

When people offer help, let them – especially when you have a newborn. Ask them to tidy up for ten minutes, pack up the recycling, bring over a pot of soup, or take your baby out of earshot so you can nap, have a shower or catch up on your paperwork. Don't be shy asking – friends will know how to say no. As your baby grows you can return the favour by offering play dates or setting up babysitting swaps.

If you or your partner can't handle a seemingly green idea, find another solution. If you are going to enjoy your eco journey it helps if you are both going along for the ride. Talk, dream and do the big changes together, and then just get on with the smaller ones. You'll be amazed at how much there is to talk about – who knows, you could add a new spark to your relationship as a result.

Going green isn't the dowdy choice; it's a fun, sassy way to help your baby and the planet have the best possible future.

Baby steps

Small

○ Make shopping lists so you only buy things you really need.

○ Suggest family/friends choose a barely used item as a baby-welcoming gift from second-hand sites like Freecycle or eBay (see list in Resources).

○ Clear a drawer, or find a large basket, tea chest or cardboard box that you can use to store your new baby's toys and books in your sitting room/kitchen (rather than an out of the way bedroom). That way you can maintain an adult, clutter-free room during the first few weeks when you may have more visitors than usual – and you'll have plenty of items on hand to entertain your baby as they start to enjoy playthings more.

Medium

○ Ask your friends what equipment they hardly ever used when they had a baby – and then borrow useful equipment and maternity clothes.

○ Decide what space you have to park a buggy. If it's really small choose a collapsible buggy.

Large

○ Start thinking about how you want to raise your baby. How much overlap is there with your partner's aspirations?

○ Give yourself enough time to find second-hand/pre-loved items. One posting on Freecycle is unlikely to turn up the exact thing that you need, or you may have to factor in extra time to collect an eBay purchase.

One
Give Your Home a Green Makeover

Most families with antenatal appointments and a snapshot of their bump cannot resist doing up a room. But do you really need all the paraphernalia that advertisers bombard you with? Is decorating a room for your baby – or it is more for you? It may seem lazy, but doing nothing except insulating your home is the best present you could give any child.

> There are thousands of plastic products on the market designed to make life easier for parents and babies. The majority of these don't make life easier, clutter our lives, cost money and end up in landfill, nappies included. We don't need everything that the advertising industry tells us. What we need is to keep it simple.
>
> Rachel, 39, with Jude, ten, and Eve, 14 months

The nesting instinct – making your home clean, safe and comfortable for your baby – is very common among new parents-to-be. Unfortunately, from the time you announce that you're expecting a new member of your family, the advertising industry – and sometimes your family and friends – bombard you with stuff they say that you must have. Sometimes it seems nesting is less about making your home fit for a baby, and more about cluttering up your life.

Instead, why not channel your energies into making your home as warm, comfortable and as draught-free as possible? As if climate change wasn't bad enough, every molecule of carbon dioxide that we burn for heating our homes or driving our cars lives on in the atmosphere for around 100 years.

Making Your Home Energy-Efficient

In 2009 government advisers reckoned it could cost you £15,000 to make your house really energy-efficient. It does sound very expensive, but your home will be so much more comfortable if it is draught-free; you will be making savings as your power bills will be correspondingly lower; the resale value of your home will increase as buyers are becoming more and more savvy about energy efficiency and you will be helping to reduce carbon emissions.

' The traditional view that people who are at home all the time will have higher fuel bills is missing the point. It's because people with young children are at home more and need higher temperatures that they need more energy-efficient homes, so that they can actually afford to keep warm. '

Andrew Myer, from Chris Barnett Associates, Energy & Environmental Consultants (and dad of Ella, nine)

Your boiler

A well-maintained, modern gas boiler, with individual controls – thermostatic radiator valves (TRVs) on each radiator and a centrally sited thermostat – can be an efficient way to keep your home warm in the cold if you take the time to get to know the controls. Match the heating hours with when you are in the house. If your child is already at nursery and you are out during the day you could set the heating so it turns off half an hour before you leave the house. You can also set it for half an hour before you normally arrive home if you like to fling your coat off when you get in – at our house we put on fleeces when we come inside. If it gets very cold try a hot-water bottle on your lap. Rugs, quilts or even duvets for snuggling under when you watch a DVD are a good way of staying warm too.

Tip

Remember to change your boiler's thermostat when the clocks change in late October and March, or if you are away for a night or longer.

Insulation and draught-proofing

We draught-proofed external doors – it was easy to get insulating strips from a hardware store. The kitchen is very cold, so between the kitchen and dining room we insulated the internal door and put a brush strip on the bottom to stop draughts. We've got a long snakey thing in front of the main door, and insulated the letter box. The living-room floor is quite draughty so we bought a thick rug to make the floor seem much cosier when the kids were crawling on it. The front room has original stained glass – which means no double glazing – so instead we got floor-to-ceiling lined curtains. We really thought about cutting down draughts because we keep the thermostat at 17°C in the winter, and the heating isn't on all day, so if you are staying in the house you wrap the kids up and put on thermal underwear. Elsie wears tights under her trousers, and a nice woolly jumper knitted by her grandmother. '

Anna, 36, with Freddie, four, and Elsie, two

A good tip if you are watching your budget is to concentrate on making the room you use most – perhaps your kitchen or living room – better insulated. Better draught-proofing may be all you need.

Turn your efforts to hunt out draughts into a game with the kids. Explain it costs money to heat space. 'Money that could be spent on fruit' is one way to motivate your assistants, whose mission is to find all the ways heat escapes from each room. Firstly organise a kit for your energy auditors with a tape measure, notebook, pen and super-sized matches. When it's breezy outside, look for draughts, flimsy window coverings, gappy floorboards and absent insulation. A good trick is to light a match to see if the flame and smoke go straight up, which means that part of your home is well draught-proofed. Pay attention when the smoke angles off at 90 degrees as that is a sign of a major draught (front and back doors are often the biggest culprits for this). Get the children to use their fingers to locate the cold stream of air, then measure the gaps so that you can make a draught excluder.

Tip

Make a doorway draught excluder from scraps

You can buy fancy designs – snakes, sausage dogs, longitudinal cityscapes – to place at the floor edge of all doors that let a draught in under them. Or you could create one yourself. If you don't want to sew, stuff a pair of a toddler's outgrown or your own raggedy woolly tights with scrumpled newspaper balls or unwanted material offcuts or cut-up, worn-out clothes. See if you can model the tights to do the splits so the doorstop will lay flat, then stop your stuffing falling out by sealing the crotch with safety pins, rubber bands or a length of rag used as a ribbon. Attach another loop of ribbon at one end so that you can hang up when not needed.

If you've got a fireplace get your children to guess what is the biggest place in the room that could remove heat (clue, it's big enough for a child to hide in). When they eventually spot it suggest fitting a chimney balloon (see Resources).

Curtains work best if they do not cover radiators and are lined. With your auditors' help, take notes so you can fix this (pinning lining material to your current curtains with safety pins or staples is an excellent quick fix if you don't have much time or budget).

Shopping list to banish draughts

At the hardware store

- ⭕ Matches
- ⭕ Brush or sponge draught excluder
- ⭕ Spongy strip window seal
- ⭕ Key and letter box covers
- ⭕ Latex wood floor filler
- ⭕ Rolls of insulating material (look for environmentally friendly options – these could include insulation made from recycled plastic bottles or even sheep's wool)

Second-hand sources (or borrow, swap, just treat yourself and buy?)

- ⭕ Old curtains, material, blankets
- ⭕ Sewing thread

Internet

- ⭕ Chimney balloon (an inflatable plug to stop heat escaping upwards)

Insulation

If you live in a house (or the top flat) insulating the attic should be a priority. All you need to do is lay insulation material thickly over your attic floor. A typical three-bedroom house will cost around £400 to insulate the attic space, but you will get an annual saving off your fuel bill of about £100 simply by not wasting so much heat through the roof. The more fuel prices go up, the better your savings. You can find out about grants and supplier information from the Energy Saving Trust but you can also buy easy-to-roll out material from DIY stores.

Super-insulation can be fitted internally, externally or between floors and is a much more messy, skilled and expensive job. However if you are doing a big building project it makes sense to spend as much as you can afford on insulation as the comfort level to your home will soar – your house will be less cold in winter and less hot in summer.

Insulating tasks

Task	Easy or difficult?	Cost?
Insulating your loft	Easy (but you'll need to clear up the attic first)	Cheap. Grants are available, the job can be staggered and the payback immediate (from reduced heating bills and improved comfort)
Jacket on your hot water tank	Easy	Low (or wrap up with an unwanted duvet/ eiderdown)
Internal wall insulation	Needs thought – add to any extension or building plans. New materials are appearing – the super-thin, super-insulating Aerogel is the great new material	Expensive if a one-off. No extra cost if part of a building project

External wall insulation	Expensive but prevents building upheavals, and you will not lose internal floor space	Pricey – though this can be reduced if neighbours network and organise as a group
Under-floor insulation	Plan when doing major works	A good green choice is Warmcel (treated and torn-up newspapers) used under suspended floors

Microgeneration

‘ I think that if children are brought up in an environmentally responsible home they are more likely to grow into adults who want to run their own homes in a similarly considerate way and that is how you create lasting change: by educating the next generation. The trouble is that there are so many options. We are looking into a wind turbine, a wood pellet boiler, solar PVs on the roof, water butts and a heat exchange system. But some of these things are so expensive and it's not clear how effective they are. Everyone has a different opinion. ’
Liz, 33, with Riley, six, and Bertie, three

Microgeneration is when individuals generate power from renewable sources such as sunlight, water and wind. Good Energy, an independent renewable energy company, has more than 650 home generators registered with them – some homes may get their energy from picturesque watermills but most people just have a couple of solar PV panels on their roof. Although solar panels are an expensive upfront purchase, using them means that you can generate the equivalent of 12 weeks of electricity each year – which you should be able to get reimbursed by your electricity provider.

Solar thermal (which enables the sun to heat up your water) is a popular renewable technology because it gives masses of free hot water when it is hot and sunny, and a limited amount in colder or very cloudy weather. On a bright May or September day the water temperature will be up to 42°C, providing plenty of hot water for washing up, bathing and showering. In August it can go up to nearly 90°C, which means you will need to add cold water.

If you cannot imagine generating your own power, perhaps because you are in a rented home, consider switching to a green energy electricity tariff, ideally one that supplies only renewable energy.

Be your own energy doctor

Now I've seen how much energy a roof kitted up with solar panels can generate from the sun, it's hard not to look at a row of homes with south- or south-west-facing roofs and wonder why these homes aren't utilising solar power. The answer is that it can be difficult to get information and the set-up costs can also be very expensive.

If you have seen *The Age of Stupid*, a campaigning film launched on a solar-powered screen in Leicester Square, London in 2009, you will already know that poorer families in some countries may need to increase their use of fossil fuels in order to improve living standards and life expectancy. It is also horrible to think that worldwide many under-fives still die from preventable diseases and a lack of clean drinking water. Those of us taking an unfair share need to take less, by making clever energy-efficiency changes now, rather than hoping someone will dream up a solution before it is too late. Governments are attempting to make some progress as the Copenhagen meeting in 2009 showed – and lots of people are behind it. In December that year nearly 50,000 people, including many families, joined a march organised by a coalition of environmental groups, trade unions, faith groups and the Women's Institute to show their support for cuts in polluting gases and climate justice. Climate change has no naughty step, but there are programmes to help your family cut your carbon dioxide emissions year on year. Go to the Resources section for more information.

' We know roughly what our carbon footprint is. It's at the lower end because we choose not to have a car, we have green energy – 100% renewable from Good Energy – have made one room snug and draught-proofed, and use washable nappies. When I talk to other parents I realise that though we don't do things that differently, I've saved huge amounts of money using washable nappies on more than one child and by being willing to accept hand-me-downs.
I mean, why wouldn't you? It makes me very nervous that in the future our children will turn around to our generation and say you had a chance to make the decisions to deal with climate change, and you didn't. At least I can say that their dad and I were trying. '
Anna, 36, with Freddie, four, and Elsie, two

Once you know your carbon footprint you have a way of measuring your progress as you cut your family's energy usage (see the Resources section for a selection of helpful sites). General carbon calculators gauge your fossil fuel use. So the less non-renewably sourced electricity you use and the less gas or fuel you burn, to heat your home or travel around, the lower your family's carbon footprint. The more demanding carbon calculators estimate the amount of energy used to make and transport food and consumer goods that you've bought recently (this is known as embedded energy), so prepare for surprises.

Be energy smart

If you're not sure what eats energy at your house try a week with a smart electric energy monitor that plugs into your main cable (near the fuse box) or an appliance to measure your power consumption. I borrowed one from the library, but they aren't expensive and can be bought from Good Energy and Natural Collection – see Resources for website details. The best electric energy monitors measure not just in kWh but also in pounds and pence so after a week of doing things you normally do you will know where your family's weak points are – and at what time. Do you wash away your expensively heated water in the power shower combing playdough out of your hair? Do you ever leave the DVD on standby after a session of *In the Night Garden*? When your friends came over did you fill the kettle right up for just two cups of raspberry leaf tea? Even without eco-gadgetry, it's surprisingly simple to make changes to your home and lifestyle that have a beneficial impact on your carbon emissions.

Without government help, upgrading energy supply lines (e.g., from offshore wind farms to the national electricity grid) it is virtually impossible for families plugged into the mains electricity supply, with the usual gadgets – TV, oven, computers, central heating – to drop below seven tonnes, even though this is still five tonnes off a sustainable level.

As few of us manage to live off-grid, it is perhaps comforting to know that you can buy energy generated exclusively by renewable power – wind, sun, wave and hydro – rather than electricity generated by coal-fired, inefficient plants. The best-known renewable energy tariffs for householders is offered by Good Energy. Ask your provider what they offer.

Tips for avoiding batteries

Batteries contain a potpourri of acids and heavy metals which makes them hard to recycle. Ask at the retailer where you bought them if they have a recycling point. Ways of avoiding batteries include:

○ Choose wind-up toys and products.
○ Buy (or ask for) a battery recycling kit and get in the habit of using it (great for bike lights).
○ Buy (or ask for) a wind-up torch – every house needs at least one just in case the power goes off. If it's dark outside you can have fun games with a toddler making shadows on the wall with your hands – mine loved shadow battles; or just put on wellies, go into the garden and do a light show.
○ Don't put in the batteries at all – your child may still enjoy playing with their new toy (or even just its box).
○ Make up games that are battery-free.

Using Water Efficiently

Over the past decade we've seen Carlisle, Leeds and Glouces-ter town centres flooding during summer. We've had some of the wettest summers ever, days with the heaviest rainfall and a burst of heat waves. Yet there are fears that by 2050 London-ers will often have to cope with 40°C spells and other extreme weather events due to climate change. Hotter weather makes plants difficult to grow and can be life-threatening for the old and very young. It also increases the risk of water shortages.

There are very simple things that we can do straight away to limit the water we use. Flushing the loo wastes a huge amount of drinking quality water. If you don't have a low-flush toilet system, you can reduce the flush volume by wrapping a brick in a plastic bag, filling plastic water bottles with water or sand, or install a Hippo (a cheap and ingenious water-saving device available online and from most water companies) in your cistern.

> I'm being ecological as a pregnant lady. Last night as I staggered to the loo in a haze of sleep I was thinking how you should not flush every time one has a pee (which can be every two hours).
> Stacy, 34, six months pregnant

Tip

Monthly savings

As the experience of pregnancy and birth can really help you lose your embarrassment gene it may be time to give a different form of sanitary protection a go. Menstrual cups collect blood that can be tipped away rather than being absorbed by a tampon or sanitary pad, both of which have to be disposed of. The cups are reusable, simple to keep clean (you use soap and hot water when in use; before their three–four-week rest you sterilise them by boiling for two minutes) and save you a fortune. They are tricky to get used to but when you do there is no going back. Menstrual cups are now available in Boots as well as online.

Not for the squeamish: Tip the blood you collect each period (about 90ml) into your compost bin as this will give a boost to your homemade, well-rotted black gold.

Tips for saving water

- Keep a topped-up bottle of tap water by your nappy-changing area.
- If it's hot give sponge baths to cool a baby or toddler rather than run a bath. Soak their sun hat and then put it back on their head so they stay cool as the water evaporates.
- Get hot toddlers to cool down by helping you water plants. They'll have more fun if you give them equipment that's the right size for them. Or adapt a one-litre plastic bottle by putting holes

in the lid (or base). At night use the paddling pool water to drench your plants.

○ Reuse bath water (by sharing or person after person), then use it to flush the loo. This is easier if the toilet is in the same room as the bath and you have a jug to decant water from the bath into a bucket. Two buckets equals one flush.

○ Fix leaky taps as the amount of water they waste is shocking.

○ Do not keep the taps running when you or your toddler brush their teeth. Show your child how to dip their toothbrush into a small cup of water rather than run the tap.

○ Ideally, only run your washing machine with full loads. Energy-efficient models (rated A or A+) use much less water.

○ If you have a building project or are updating a sink or bath fit spray taps which reduce the water flow.

○ Use a planet-friendly washing-up liquid (e.g., Ecover or other brands) so that when the washing up water has cooled you can pour on to garden plants (perhaps not your vegetables). Or use the water used to steam veg as a nutritious watery soup on to indoor plants – make sure that it's cooled down first. Cups of drinking water left unfinished after a meal can go the same way. Water used to clean vegetables can be tipped on thirsty plants.

○ Clean gutters and install water butts to collect water from your roof, bay window and sheds. When you are pottering in the garden you can let your toddler use this water for cooking games, mud pie games, watering the plant games, etc.

○ To help safeguard wildlife whatever the weather, leave out water for the birds and create a mini wetland or pond area. Ponds can be serious hazards for young children so fence off until your children – and visitors' children – are old enough to play safely in a garden with a pond.

Your Baby's Room

'The baby inspired us to make changes. Charlie's room is in a bit of the house that is Grade 2 listed so the thermal values were minimal – it was fairly warm in the summer and the coldest room in the house in the winter. It used to be our spare room, so we didn't use it much, and our room, in the extension, was built to newer standards. I spent an afternoon reinsulating the roof space above the ceiling of his room. I also put draught excluders on his windows and reflective backs to the radiators. We also renovated the sash windows so they could open at the top and bottom to create a through draught in the summer. It took a bit of effort but it's made a massive improvement. '
Oliver, 33, with Charlie, 18 months

For anything connected with preparing your house for a baby – and making it comfortable enough for you to spend maternity leave in it, whatever the weather – green principle number one is to make less waste. Even so, before your baby arrives, or very soon after, you will need to find space for them to sleep; to wash and dry extra laundry; to store equipment that will be used several times a day soon (such as a high chair, buggy); to store occasionally used equipment as well as the baby's clothes and toys. With this plethora of equipment, it is no wonder people's homes seem suddenly overcrowded.

Rethinking home

The solution can be a large building project or rejigging the way you use your room as the quotes from these two mums below show:

' We spent six months with the three of us living in one bedroom through the building work (including replacing a boiler, installing double-glazed windows, etc.) but we have now moved into the newly insulated bedrooms and have the joy of sleeping in warm rooms in the knowledge that we're not wasting energy and our money. We are doing a bit to helping combat climate change, and we're also adding to the value of the house because buyers increasingly look for energy-efficiency performance as a key criteria for a new home. '
Elaine, 44, with Finn, two, and Niall, two weeks

' We have a two-bedroom flat and because we are all sleeping together we still have a spare room – but after a year I found it was more like a laundry room and that annoyed me. So we put a creel [aka Sheila Maid or pulley dryer] up above the stairs and it transformed our life. We now have our spare room back and the two clothes horses are never needed, even though I wash nappies every couple of days. '
Jo, 34, with Billy, 17 months

Your home is probably fine as it is for a baby, which is good news because the greenest action you can do (besides insulation and basic energy saving) is to save resources by not doing any special decoration. But if you think this makes a poor welcome for your new family member, below are some thrifty tips for decorating their room. Making a room too baby-centric will mean that you have to redecorate all too soon. Instead, try to:

○ Draw your own or buy sheets of cheerfully designed wrapping paper (e.g., E. H. Shepard's illustrations of Winnie the Pooh), frame and hang. You can often pick up frames in charity shops.

○ Paint your own design (or copy a picture from a story book you love) directly on to the wall. Ideas that look great and could work from babyhood to the teen years include a jungle scene, landscape or a giant map of the world.

○ Let your baby share your bed and/or bedroom so you don't need to redecorate with whimsical nursery characters.

○ Repaint walls in a baby gender-neutral colour.

○ Always choose paint containing zero or minimal VOC (volatile organic compounds – look on the tin to be sure).

○ You will need lots of storage. Clear-lidded boxes that slide under beds, stack up or fit into an existing wardrobe will help you keep control of the piles of outgrown, fitting and to-grow-into garments. You can also use spare boxes for toys and washable nappies.

○ Take photos during the baby's first year and convert into art (easy to do using Photoshop or at SnappySnaps) or simply frame your favourites and display rather than keep everything that reminds you of their infant stage.

Paint

Your paint choice doesn't have to be a toxic brew of chemical colours. Some specialist companies even promise that you can compost the leftovers. Next-best selection is a paint which is clearly marked as having no VOCs (volatile organic

Lead paint

Lead is a poisonous ingredient that is known to harm young children and babies (even before they are born) by slowing growth and damaging their nervous system. Lead was commonly added to paint before 1978. If you have a home built before this year be extremely careful about redecoration, particularly when it comes to sanding down paint or stripping wallpaper. Paint over surfaces you have concerns about, and if they are in good enough condition regularly wash surfaces that might have been painted in lead-based paint, such as windowsills. Always distract or prevent children from chewing paintwork and get them to wash their hands often, especially during the fist-in-mouth stage of teething.

You can buy a lead paint test kit from DIY stores. Ideally, don't do tasks like stripping or sanding down an old cot or a window frame if you are pregnant, also keep children out of the room and be sure to wear a face mask.

Lead paint scares aren't over: there have been repeated recalls of Chinese-made toys manufactured for well-known brands because lead paint has been used. As a result it is hard to keep track of what's safe or not so if you are buying toys from a charity shop or second-hand stall (or indeed, new) make it a family rule that your child should not chew their toys. If your child is at a very chewy age, then offer something to chew that you know is safe.

compounds) or minimal (0–0.29%) VOCs on the label. Choose paint marked with minimal VOCs rather than low if you can find it in the right colour.

Inexperienced decorators tend to buy too much paint. Work out the surface area, and how many coats you will need, before you buy a five-litre pot. Label the pot and store so you can use for any touch-up jobs if your child scribbles her name on the walls in a moment of exuberant toddlerdom. If you hope to install double-glazed windows you will need to retouch the area around the frame. Half-full tins can be offered for use at nurseries, playgroups or primary schools, donated to your nearest Scrapstore (www.scrapstore.co.uk), or given away on websites such as Freecycle.

Even paints made from natural ingredients have a long lifetime so if a couple of years later you need to touch up paintwork after the suggested use-by date, try stirring vigorously to combine the separate parts into gloop again. If this doesn't work and your paint choice can be composted then remove the lid, wait for the paint to crumble dry (this may take several days) and then add to your compost heap. See Resources to source compostable paints.

Best and worst paints

Best
Compostable, clay-or plant-
(mineral) based paint with no VOCs
Minimal VOC
Low VOC
High VOC
Lead paint
Worst

Flooring

Floors follow fashion but the best choice is usually what you already have, especially if it is a smooth surface such as floorboards, but it will depend on your family's home and health. For example, an all-wool, non-synthetic backed carpet, or big rug, may help keep your room warmer and in future years also muffle the sound of early morning playing. This is a definite plus in flats if there is limited sound or heat insulation between floors and you want to keep on good terms with the neighbours downstairs. However, all carpets harbour dust mites (their poo is a known trigger for common allergies, eczema and asthma). Carpets also provide a trap for cat and pet allergens and may be left with trace coatings of VOCs and pesticides brought in from outside on pet paws and shoes. It's wise to make carpeted bedrooms out of bounds for family pets. Even super-conscientious vacuuming won't remove all the dust and dust-mite faeces in a carpet and the process stirs up dust into the room.

That's why people often damp-dust surfaces (just wet a cloth in a sink, then wring out and start wiping) and opt for

Best and worst floor choices

Best
Sand existing floorboards
    Install reclaimed boards (hard to find)
        Install FSC-certified floorboards or wood laminate
            Use linoleum or marmoleum (avoid PVC)
                Pick an all-wool carpet/rug
                    Synthetic carpet
                        PVC flooring
                            Worst

smooth floor surfaces, such as wood or lino. All wool carpets and rugs (and clothes) may also be ruined by moths – to prevent an infestation, once a year clean behind cupboards and other dark places, wipe out drawers and check you have cedar wood balls/sachets in wardrobes.

Lighting

Dim light is lovely to feed a baby by, especially when you want them to drop off to sleep, but a decent bright light will help lessen eye strain when you cut hair or read a story-book. You may find that it is more energy-efficient (and easier to read by) to use an anglepoise light in rooms that are lit by a central ceiling fitment with two or more bulbs. Homebirth mums are usually required to have one of these anyway to make the midwife's task a little better lit. Now-adays you can even find energy-efficient bulbs suitable for ceiling inset halogen lights, see www.megaman.uk.com and also www.lightbulbs-direct.com.

Shelves and storage

Auctions, attics, antique shops, junk shops, junk yards, garage sales, tabletop sales, friends and Freecycle are all ways to find storage solutions, rather than buying new. Remember to label whatever you put away. I still have baby toys in the attic which should have been given away but weren't because the bag was wrongly labelled.

If you are buying new timber look for the FSC label because Forest Stewardship Council certification guarantees that the wood has been sourced from a well-managed forest, and that it is not an illegally felled hardwood as so much rain-forest timber used to be. If you are able, buy timber from a local woodland, which will help support a local business.

Try, if you can, to avoid MDF. MDF is made from powdered wood, which is then bonded together with resin and made into boards. While MDF is often treated to be fire-, water- and stain-resistant, it can contain toxic agents such as formaldehyde, which can trigger asthma, dermatitis and is potentially carcinogenic. There is also concern that MDF may 'off-gas', i.e., slowly leak toxins into the air. And, if you are cutting MDF then be sure it is cut outside by someone wearing a face mask. Once in place air the room really well (ideally several weeks) and paint over the MDF to seal. Do not put MDF items near or above a working radiator as heat causes off-gassing.

Best DIY shelves

Best
Adapt what you already have or can find (but not using MDF)
Reuse reclaimed timber
Buy FSC-certified timber
Use recycled materials (e.g., bottle top counter)
Use FSC-certified timber mixes, e.g., ply
Use timber from unknown sources
Use MDF
Worst

Heating

Thankfully, climate change hasn't taken our summers above 40°C (106°F) yet, but it can still make homes far too hot.

Children with eczema are likely to be set off scratching in over-heated, stuffy, carpeted rooms. Insulation keeps rooms at comfortable temperatures, whatever the weather.

Tips for keeping babies cool

- Move your baby's sleeping space out of direct sunlight.
- If you are lucky enough to have outdoor space with a tree could your child safely sleep under cool, dappled sunlight in their buggy occasionally (with you nearby)? If you are using a sunshade remember that you will need to change the angle as the sun moves westwards or just drape muslins over the pram/buggy hood.
- Think like a southern European and close the curtains when the sun beams directly through single- or double-glazed windows, especially between 11 a.m.–2 p.m.
- Encourage a through draught from one side of your home to the other by opening windows or doors on opposite sides of your house. Use sash windows correctly by opening at both the top and bottom to create a through draught.
- Open your attic hatch so that hot air can rise above your living and sleeping spaces.
- Add shutters to windows that are hit by direct sun, or grow a sun-loving plant up that wall, such as passion fruit or a grapevine.
- Remove rugs and thick curtains (this is a good time to clean and store them) and free the chimney balloon.

The ideal sleeping temperature for an infant is in the range of 16–20°C; the Energy Saving Trust recommends setting your daytime thermostat at the lowest comfortable temperature – between 18–21°C. If you add a jumper or two to you and your baby's outfits, you'll find that turning down your thermostat won't make your home feel like a chiller cabinet. And if it does then you are being given a clear signal that your home needs to be better insulated.

Tips for keeping babies and toddlers warm

○ Over-sized tops with long sleeves keep hands and wrists warmer and are easier to use than gloves. Roll up the sleeves when your baby wakes or wants to play. Or pop mittens (or socks) on to your infant's hands. Avoid losing gloves by putting a pair on to a long elastic and thread through the sleeves of outdoor coats. If you have no heating you can also put an extra pair of socks over or under an all-in-one, or add a soft cotton, or thicker, woolly hat.

○ Dress your baby in two pairs of trousers, or tights and trousers, which will trap a warm air layer next to the skin – just like wearing thermals.

○ In your house (in addition to draught-proofing) cover smooth surfaced floors with a rug or playmat in winter; draw curtains at dusk; don't place furniture in front of radiators. Consider adding another lining to your curtains (do this quickly by stapling, safety pinning or sewing on a made up set of curtains found in a charity shop). If you have blinds try to also use curtains during the winter.

○ Save energy and money by keeping just one room really cosy and warm.

'My mum brings an extra coat when she comes to stay because she says my home is freezing in winter, about 16°C. But you toughen up and we do keep the bathrooms warmer. I didn't use sleep sacks with the girls, and they all kicked off their covers, so I always put them to bed in an all-in-one and cardy.'

Tara, 37, with Olivia, ten, Eve, seven, and Orla, four

Safety

'You have to be really organised when you've got toddlers and not leave things lying around, like scissors or cleaning products. But I didn't bother with stair gates – I live in a three-storey house with lots of stairs so thought it would be better for the children to get used to using the stairs safely. Also, as my eldest got older she might have been able to open the gates, but then not shut them, which would mean her little brother would fall. Alfie started climbing the stairs at eight months, before he could walk. He loved it and still spends hours doing it.'

Sarra, 36, with Saskia, four, Alfie, two, and Ivan, three months

Babies' ability to move around and do stuff changes so fast that the only way to keep up is to be more like them. Once they are five or six months (or just starting to roll over) get on your hands and knees and crawl around your home to work out what tempting dangers will soon be at their eye level – plug sockets, trailing wires and even pins. If cupboards can be opened by a baby, they may find brightly coloured bottles containing cleaning chemicals or medication which could lead to accidental poisoning. Ideally, move these things on to higher shelves and when used up replace with less toxic brands.

Whether you decide to use safety gates, window restrictors, non-slip bath/shower mats, fire guards, kitchen cupboard/drawer locks and, when they are first walking, pads on sharp corners (e.g., kitchen units, tables) will depend on your attitude to risk. Do you tend towards the gung-ho? Can you learn to shush your in-built worry alarm and let young children learn to judge their own limits? I forgave myself for worrying about my first child a lot, but also tried to let her have as much independence as she was physically capable of. So she was soon climbing into her wooden high chair, feeding herself with her fingers and spoon and enjoying walking on low walls out and about. You can apply this have-a-go principle to most things related to children – as they start getting teeth you can encourage them to clean them and then help out with the tricky bits or once they can use a potty or loo themselves they can also wipe their bum (rather than expect you to do it).

> I'm going to put the mattress on the floor, it was so horrible when J rolled off the bed and we had to go to A&E again. I feel like we are on first-name terms at the hospital after all my trips up there.
> Anonymous mum with two young children

It's obvious that you really shouldn't drop your baby, but a large number of under-six-month-old babies are rushed to hospital because they suddenly roll off the sofa, bed or nappy-changing table that they'd been safely using until that particular incident. It will happen to you too unless you take care. Make sure anyone who helps you with the baby regularly is alert to the way your child is developing.

Avoid falls by putting your mattress on the floor or switching to a futon. Or if you are co-sleeping, lay your child on the wall/cot side, or roll up a towel tightly so that it wedges your child away from the edge.

Anticipating a fall is a good enough reason to change your baby's nappy on the floor – that way you can turn your back to put the dirty nappy into a bucket or bin, dampen a flannel and collect a clean nappy without having to panic that your little one is about to make her first roll-over with disastrous consequences.

Take special care

Plug sockets and air fresheners

You can pop on plug safety covers for unused plugs to stop the risk of electrocution when a baby forces their damp fingers into the skirting board.

Be wary of parfum, as it is a synthetic ingredient in many perfumes and scented products despite being an allergy trigger for millions, so while your baby is young do them a favour and keep it out of your house – why take the risk? Rather than try to disguise a bad smell with an unhealthy product or a plug-in air freshener, open the window, or grow and cut your own sweet-smelling flowers (e.g., sweet peas, roses, hyacinth).

Sharp corners

New walkers move erratically and often crash into hard objects. If they are pushing a trolley or mini buggy this might stave off a headlong bash, but it's no guarantee. Ideally keep a close watch and the floor as clear as possible so your toddler doesn't have to cope with trip hazards. Some families tape rolls of newspaper to corners. You can just about get away with minimal redecoration if you use masking tape to secure.

DIY materials (e.g., paints, varnish and glue), garden sprays, kitchen cleaners and medicines

All need to be kept out of reach or in a locked cupboard. It is particularly important not to decant poisons into bottles that children recognise (e.g., do not put paint stripper into an old lemonade bottle). Slug pellets look like blue sweeties to children and lindane – a common ingredient in ant killer until it was banned (but can still be found in garden sheds) – looks like the sweet powder from a sherbert dib dab. Hopefully your children will know not to eat 'sweets' they find lying around, but it would be less risky if you didn't use these chemicals in your garden. Far better for wildlife too.

Teflon

It is impossible not to worry about what chemicals you are feeding unintentionally as you heat up your child's dinner. Unhappy about the long-term health risks of using Teflon coatings, I got rid of my non-stick pans for a while (via a charity shop). I now have just one in the house which is used to make pancakes. I hope this is an example of the precautionary principle used pragmatically – I mostly avoid Teflon coatings, but occasionally it's perfect for the task.

Microwaves

> I don't own a microwave and don't trust them. If we go out to tea I ask for my girls' food to be heated up in a pan or let them eat it cold. I've found people don't really fuss about this if I explain. I'm sure they use microwaves in restaurants but I try to ignore this.
>
> Tara, 37, with Olivia, ten, Eve, seven, and Orla, four

Although microwaves are brilliant at using minimal amounts of energy to cook food, many parents avoid using them. Food and drinks can be easily reheated on the hob or an energy-efficient fan oven – there's plenty of space to heat up several different dishes for 20–30 minutes at 180°C. You may not even need to turn the oven on as many dishes can be enjoyed cold, including milk/formula. Food can be carried around in glass containers, or if you need to provide your baby with lunch at a childminder's or nursery, pack carefully into a glass jar inside a shatterproof plastic sealed box ready to be decanted and heated up.

Culturally, we think a hot meal in the middle of the day is important for little ones, but this might stem from a time when there was no central heating or good waterproof clothing and people did much more physically demanding jobs outside. Try serving cold pasta salads, sandwiches, boiled or baked potatoes, dips and pitta bread, cereals, fresh fruit, hard-boiled eggs, cold cooked veg (sweetcorn, potato, beans), slices of omelette, chicken, ham, cheese chunks, fish, etc.

Switched on to microwaves?

> The "environmental issue" which has really stressed me is whether I'm poisoning Anna by microwave reheating her food in plastic bowls. The compromise I've come to is to only use microwave-safe bowls (which are marked with a symbol of a square with wiggly lines through it), and to only warm the food, rather than heating it to boiling.

Sally, 38, with Anna, two

The jury is still out – which side will you take?

POSITIVES:

Microwaves use less energy and make cooking and reheating food (in microwave-safe bowls) extremely quick, which is as good for our power bills as it is for time-pressed parents. You could also speed up your own cooking by using an ultra efficient induction hob, use lids on all saucepans and or make more use of a pressure cooker.

NEGATIVES:

Microwaves leak electromagnetic radiation, destroy nutrients in foods and scramble food molecules, possibly creating toxic side effects.

Wi-fi and mobile phones

It is too early to know the effect of wi-fi and mobile phone use on human health. However, you might want to avoid letting your baby or toddler speak on mobile phones as a result of research from Friends of the Earth Scotland (see Bibliography for details):

> If there are currently unrecognised adverse health effects from the use of mobile phones, children may be more vulnerable because of their developing nervous system, the greater absorption of energy in the tissues of the head (paragraph 4.37), and a longer lifetime of exposure. In line with our precautionary approach, at this time, we believe that the widespread use of mobile phones by children for non-essential calls should be discouraged. We also recommend that the mobile phone industry should refrain from promoting the use of mobile phones by children (paragraphs 6.89 and 6.90).

It is easy to fob off a baby/toddler with a toy mobile, make a mini cereal packet into their own mobile or just give them an unwanted model with the battery and SIM card removed.

Brominated flame retardants (BFRs)

BFRs have been used for around 30 years to stop fire spreading so fast. They are applied to soft furnishings, mattresses, foam, sofas, easy chairs, and electronics, including PCs and TVs. BFRs are toxic industrial chemicals which have managed to enter the food chain and are known to have adverse health effects. They do this by shape-changing enough to end up in house dust, where they can be easily consumed either on sticky fingers or as a surface BFR-laced dust resting on unwashed or other types of food. It is recommended that you keep soft furnishings in good condition – so if there is a split, mend it and also fix the covers in order to stop the spread of dust around the house. During the crawling stage wash your baby's hands regularly with soap and water, especially before they eat.

Cleaning your home

Because babies are growing so fast, and their brain keeps on developing even when they are out of the womb, you need to keep your home as toxic free as you can. Do this by trying to choose products that don't compromise your home's air quality.

Tips

Make a cleaning spritzer

To shift daily grime on kitchen surfaces mix white vinegar with tap water. Keep in an unused plant mister (or washed-out cleaning spray bottle) and use when you want to clean surfaces. If you want a stronger mix just add more vinegar.

Lemon for limescale

You can use lemon juice (fresh or bottled) as a base in a spritzer but this keeps less well, and needs to be rinsed off so may be better suited for regular jobs like cleaning taps and sinks.

Remove odours

Buy a large packet of bicarbonate of soda (available from chemists) and sprinkle liberally over items that smell – a genius way to remove the smell of vomit if your child is travel sick.

Ideally, replace the products in your cleaning arsenal that are damaging to water and use antibacterials sparingly. You can make natural cleaning products to clean floors, and surfaces. Instead of bleaches and harsh cleaners that sting your hands you can use better cleaning cloths with microfibres that can help loosen dirt in an almost magical way.

To prevent the spread of dust, go easy on vacuuming, instead start by damp dusting surfaces and gradually remove carpets which can become reservoirs of all sorts of nasties, including allergens. Useful, non-toxic cleaning products are lemon juice (use to shift marks, add a fresh scent, remove ingrained dirt – but remember to rinse well), bicarbonate of soda and vinegar (which also removes limescale deposits in kettles). If you don't wish to give up your favourite brands just try using the tips shown opposite.

Lots of cleaning equipment gets thrown out after one use, but, sponges, jay cloths, microcloths and dusters can all be made good (for a while) in the washing machine. Worn-out clothes can be cut up and used as rags. Old nailbrushes and toothbrushes can become cleaning equipment for hard-to-reach areas too.

Try to avoid

Baby wipes: used once then binned. Try making your own (see chapter 5, p.140).

Battery-operated toothbrushes: a child needs help cleaning their own teeth until they are seven so give them your help rather than a toothbrush which will soon need its batteries replaced.

Battery-powered thermometers: they have a two-year lifespan and then need to be replaced. In contrast, non-digital thermometers can last a lifetime.

Buying new cleaning products when the bottle runs out: can you find a brand that can be refilled, and a shop near you that does this? Or buy in bulk and share with friends.

Throwing out dirty cloths: soak in a bucket overnight and then wash with other dirty items.

Insulating your home, using water efficiently, keeping your house cool and adding extra layers of clothing when it's cold, using energy-efficient methods to power your home, avoiding toxic chemicals when decorating or cleaning your home – all of these are simple steps you can take which will lay the foundations for a happy and healthy childhood – and life – for your baby.

Baby steps

Small

○ Support renewable energy companies by buying your electricity and gas from them. Sign up to the weekly email prompt from Act on CO_2 (see Resources for website information).

○ Turn your thermostat down one degree and keep a big rug to snuggle under when you read or watch telly.

○ Talk to people about what they've done in their house to be more energy efficient. Has it been hard to do?

Medium

○ Even if you've signed up to the 10:10 campaign, look at the Energy Saving Trust website and work through the tips: www.est.co.uk.

○ Make the room you spend most time in cosier. Prioritise blocking up draughts. Think doors, windows, floorboards, skirting boards, chimneys, ceiling.

○ Aim to make your house a model of energy efficiency.

○ Borrow or buy an energy meter that clips on to your main electricity input wire and can tell you exactly how much power your house is using, as well as the cost.

Large

○ Find a friend to be your energy buddy and while your babies are amusing each other (or asleep) get together to identify places heat leaks so you can decide what needs insulating.

○ Try joining an eco-club (see Resources).

○ Consider triple glazing, triple insulating walls, etc. Look for tips and grants at Energy Saving Trust.

○ Consider the need to cool your house some months, as well as capture heat.

○ Set aside some time to measure your carbon footprint so you can find ways to reduce the amount of energy you use. Then start reducing your carbon emissions each year.

Two
Shopping

It's not just new ways of shopping you can try, there's also a lot of swapping to be done. To keep costs and clutter down, find out what equipment other new parents felt worked well, and try to borrow what you can. Always be on the lookout for items that you can recondition or repair. This isn't as hard as it may sound: once you have a baby you will find yourself belonging to a network of clubs which are attended by resourceful, informative parents and childminders – many of whom know someone who is keen to get rid of outgrown necessities. And if you absolutely have to buy new, make sure that you choose a supplier who manufactures their goods in an ethically responsible way.

'You feel it's a new baby so everything's got to be perfect. You see people buying brand new and because you don't know anything you think you've got to do that too. But you don't need to – especially if you'd never normally buy that many new things all in one go. Someone's always got one you can borrow, just to try it out. Or they may want to give it away. Or you can buy second-hand. But I think part of the pleasure of buying less is that you can make so many things – lovely clothes and sweet toys. My friend made Faith a felt crown. It's really nice for her dressing-up box. I think having homespun things helps children realise that they can make things too; it's an early lesson in not consuming. **'**

Pip, 46, and Faith, three

Changing the way we buy, reuse or recondition things is a key part of green thinking. If we can borrow what we can, search out the items that we need in charity shops or websites such as Freecycle, and buy locally or ethically sourced products, then we will be helping the environment, as well as our wallets.

It's estimated that parents spend as much as £9,500 on their baby in their child's first year. That's scary stuff, and scarier still if you think that most of this £9,500 is spent on luxuries, not necessities, for the baby. The fact is that you don't need everything that advertisers want you to buy, or at least not always new and probably not just yet. Of course most stores want us spending our money (in these credit crunch times it's almost considered patriotic) and they make sure that baby basics – from high chairs to cots – are made more temptingly affordable by limited-offer discounts. Once you're shopping – in store or online – they'll display lots of other baby paraphernalia to tempt you with. The result is new mums and dads look as if we are the folk born yesterday.

Equipment you just won't need

○ **High chairs** at every house you spend time at. An alternative is a cloth baby seat that can be taken with you when you visit friend's homes or a café without a high chair. Or use a quick adjustable table seat that screws on to some tables. Better still, pop your baby on your lap – or leave them in the buggy.

- ○ **Splash mat** – just mop up food, drink and craft spills direct from the table or floor. Make your life easier by only serving food in one room – or over a non-carpeted area of a room.
- ○ **Plastic cutlery** – let your baby experiment with his hands and then use teaspoons or small cutlery.
- ○ **China baby plate, bowl and mug set** – use and you will need to concentrate every second as the dropping game is irresistible until children are about three years old. Got one already? Then use as crocks/drainage in plant pots when it does break.
- ○ **Baby monitor** – only needed for larger homes or for those parents with hearing problems. Try leaving the baby's door open before acquiring your own monitor.
- ○ **Baby sleeping bags** that zip up the side so that your little baby cannot kick off the blankets. Brand new, these are not a budget buy, especially as you will need two of each size in case your baby's nappy leaks or there is some other disaster. Babies wake up just as often in baby sleeping bags as they do using a sheet/blanket, so don't think this is the definitive answer to getting a whole night's sleep. It's not.

'I've been using the library rather than buying baby books. I've also rediscovered the books and toys in storage at my parents' house from my own childhood. My little boy is going to have a lot to welcome him!'
Stacy, 34, eight months pregnant

Before your infant darling arrives, consider whether you (or someone else) can adapt what you already have. For instance, many families use a drawer (removed from a chest of drawers) instead of a Moses basket, which is only used for a very short amount of time in your baby's life. Instead of a **baby nest** (a doughnut-shaped ring) use a cardboard box with strategically placed cushions.

Pimp my buggy blanket

Here's an idea for a unique design that helps your child stay warm and gives you a warm glow of achievement when you see it in use.

○ Find an unworn or too-scruffy-to-be-worn thick fleece jacket (look in the back of your cupboard or at a car boot sale). Cut to the size you want. You can avoid hemming the edges if you cut with pinking shears. Hemming is a good idea, though.

○ Decorate with a contrasting fleece using a shape that you've cut out from an unwanted top and sew on. Keep your first design simple. Or you can sew or iron on badges found in museum shops or more delicate motifs sold in craft shops. Or how about sewing on a design your family loves filched from an unwanted T-shirt?

If you can't adapt, try to buy second-hand. Charity shops are a good place to find many things your baby needs, but don't limit yourself to the local goodwill. Second-hand items can be found in many places – try and buy brand-new items as a last resort.

Practical gifts

If anyone offers to get something for your baby – and soon-to-be grandparents may want to be generous – the items below are really useful. Your gift-giver may prefer to get them new, but most can also be sourced second-hand.

○ V- or U-shaped pillow (with washable cover). A big pillow can make breastfeeding at home more comfortable by allowing you to lay your baby closer to your breast. Piling up pillows/cushions or tightly rolling up a towel can work just as well.

○ Easy-to-carry travel changing mat and nappy pack (a diaper bag) so you can change your baby in the park or simply use if conditions are wet or not as clean as you'd like.

○ Light, collapsible buggy that fits through your door and in your hallway.

○ Bits and bobs for the buggy such as a waterproof cover or possibly a sun shade, but this isn't needed if you have a hood as you can always face the buggy away from the sun or walk on the shady side of the street/path.

○ Outdoor gear, which includes a warm hat or a sun hat depending on the season, waterproof crawler suit, too-big jacket or all-in-one body suit so that hands can be covered.

○ Hand-held food mixer that can be used to make purées, remove lumps, create soups, etc.

○ Adjustable high chair. Some can be folded up when not in use, others, like the wooden Stokke Tripp Trapp, can be used long after your child leaves primary school – in fact the blurb says they are OK until your child reaches 18 stone (which, hopefully, they won't!). If you want to have family meals with everyone eating around the table choose a high chair that doesn't take up too much leg space and looks as if it will be robust.

○ Plastic no-leak cup and lid (this is your treat: it will allow your baby to play without you having to mop up spills constantly).

Borrowing etiquette

It's a good idea to make a written note of who lends you what, and what they'd like you to do with it when your child has outgrown it. Prams and cots can be expensive so it may not be appropriate to pass it on without checking with the original owner first. When you borrow an item, ask if they'll want you to give it back, pass it on, keep for next child, sell it and split the money, sell it and give all the money to the first owner (or donate to a good cause).

I asked as many friends as possible with children if they have anything I can borrow. In fact, I haven't really needed to ask. Everyone has offered. I've said yes constantly – with no shame. It's great and I hopefully will do the same when I've had number one and before a second child (if we get that far).

Jo, baby due in two weeks

Finding pre-loved items

I work as a childminder and try to live a green lifestyle. I have used washable nappies, got a double buggy off Freecycle, bought second-hand clothes and often give away clothes to other mums.

Jo, 39, with Ben, five, and Sally, two

Children grow bigger so fast that it saves cash finding pre-loved items. Sharing special items, or even the basics, is a lovely way to connect a family or friends. And it is also an imaginative and neighbourly way to pass on your own things. Possessions may come with a story, affection or – best of all – personal recommendations.

The girls wear the clothes that I used to wear, lovely smock dresses and even the pyjamas that my mother kept – there were quite a few boxes. I'm doing the same for my future grandchildren. I keep favourite toys, books and special clothes. I've got photo albums of me having an Easter egg hunt with my grandmother when I was little and my daughters can recognise that I'm wearing their dress! It's lovely for my family having everything passed through the generations, but it also brings back memories for all my friends who remember wearing similar dresses.

Tara, 37, with Olivia, ten, Eve, seven, and Orla, four

If you can't find what you want from the usual suspects then there are a vast number of places you may be able to buy what you are looking for cheaply. You may find an infant and toddler clothes swap being run near you. Sure Start (see Resources for more information) and children's centres are a good place to start; charity shops are great, and if you regularly look through their stock you will probably be lucky finding what you want. Also try specialist second-hand baby clothing shops, charity shops, nearly-new and table-top sales (check the NCT website for events near you at www.nct.org.uk/in-your-area/nearly-new-sales). There is also the excitement of finding exactly what you need at jumble and car boot sales, school fetes and yard sales. If you are bold enough you could even hold a recycled items only baby shower by asking friends to bring or lend you items and equipment they no longer need, but think you will find useful.

'I never used a toy library as such but treated our local charity shops in much the same way. Unless you are totally committed, the rising tide of plastic crap seems to be inevitable...'

Gaby, 36, with Barney, nine, and Toby, four

Make you own for sale / give away / wanted list

At places parents and babies gather you may find the coordinator or an organised parent has drawn up a chart that offers families the chance to swap, buy or give away equipment. If you want to do this make it robust enough to carry around with you and smart enough to pop on the table during the group (look at café menu displays for inspiration). If you are new to the group ask the person running the group if they'd mind a list being left on display. Here's an example of a list used at a homebirth group that meets in a park café once a week.

For sale – give away – wanted

Please add your details and cross off if sold/taken/no longer required

Item description	For sale/ gift/ wanted	Cost if applicable	Name	Telephone or email contact
Nursery curtains. Unused animal farm theme	Gift, free	N/a (you need to collect)		
Play mat/ baby gym	Wanted			
La Bassine birthing pool	For sale	£60		
Bath and nursing pillow	Free			
Moses basket	Unwanted gift	Free		

Tip

Before you start searching charity shops, make a list of the items you want in the sizes you need and keep the list in your purse or wallet. That means you won't forget the things you need.

The Cambridge branch of the NCT runs a popular nearly-new sale every October that raises around £12,000 for maternal and infant projects and allows parents to pass things on, snap up just what they wanted and generally enjoy getting together. Nearly-new sales are not just a system that's good for your purse and fundraising for maternal health, they are also combating waste in the world by giving outgrown and unwanted items a new lease of life instead of being consigned to landfill.

You probably know your way around eBay already, and if you sell things you no longer need on eBay, you could fund

Shopping and swapping

Sites that offer free and/or good value items/conversation/ideas, enabling you to find the exact items you need, include:

- Craigslist: www.craigslist.co.uk
- eBay online auctions: www.ebay.co.uk
- Freecycle – join your local group and benefit from all the items offered close to your home. Also good for getting rid of things you no longer want. www.freecycle.org
- Gumtree: www.gumtree.com (check out the freebies)
- Ooffoo – set up by the Natural Collection, encourages a community feel by letting users swap know-how, sell things and share good ideas: www.ooffoo.com
- NCT forum: www.nationalchildirthtrust.com
- SwapXchange: www.swapxchange.org (often linked to council websites)
- You can also try setting up informal offers/wanted requests on office or neighbourhood email lists.

the purchase of the next item on your list; whereas users of www.ooffoo.com may find their search for new ways of kitting their kids might draw them into a cyber conversation that offers a huge range of ideas, and – whisper it – shopping opportunities. And you can always ask people – you are sure to uncover talent or find an interesting alternative that would do just as well.

> We are using slings made by a friend's mum. We are using the bathroom sink to bathe Gabriel, as well as bathing with him. We have a "nappy change table" but it's a table we will use for something else once he has grown out of nappies; and other than clothes, that's pretty much it.
>
> Emma, 34, with Gabriel, seven weeks

Reconditioning, repairing and passing on

All round the UK there are repair shops, skilled craftspeople and mechanics. Finding a good Mr Fix It is not easy, and you never know what you want until an unexpected break happens so jot down numbers, websites, contacts when you see them or ask for recommendations from friends, family and neighbours. Googling the craft you need and your postcode can help turn up surprising repair outfits from buggy mechanics to someone able to patch up the antique nursing chair you've just inherited.

With a new baby you probably won't be doing too much DIY but you could put together a basic repair pack and have a go fixing things. You'll need:

○ Tape measure

○ Sandpaper – smoothes down splintery edges, can help to remove heat stains

○ Awl – so you can easily screw hooks into wood and start off a nail more successfully

○ Hammer, Phillips screwdriver, ordinary screwdriver, Allan key

○ Spirit level – to make things straight

○ Jars of mixed sizes for screws, nails, etc.

○ Battery recharger so you don't have to keep on chucking out (or attempting to recycle) spent batteries

Besides Freecycle, you can also offload furniture and electrical items that you don't want any more on to your nearest Furniture Reuse Network depot. This organisation passes on good quality and reconditioned items to people who really need them. Donating your unwanted fridge is a triple win: you get rid of something you no longer want, you know that it won't go to landfill and it will be used by someone who really needs it. FRN employs more than 3,000 staff and provides training for more than 8,000, supports more than 10,000 volunteers, helps around 700,000 low-income households and ensures that 2.5 million items each year avoid landfill. See more, including their latest campaign The Big Womble, a name borrowed from the eponymous children's book by Elisabeth Beresford, at www.frn.org.uk.

Broken electrical items – such as that horrible fluorescent light in the kitchen, your stepson's broken Nintendo DS, your old PC and even worn-out energy-efficient light bulbs – are known as waste electrical and electronic equipment (WEEE). Paul Bonomini's seven-metre robotic giant, made from the

3.3 tonnes of electrical scrap that is estimated each of us in the UK will throw away during our lifetimes, graphically illustrates just how wasteful our lives can be. See the pictures at http://weeeman.org. If you've got something broken, you can find an electrical waste collection point close to where you live that will help you dispose of broken items correctly at www.easyweee.com.

Tip

New life for old cots

Wire cot bases and dismantled wooden cot sides can be given a new role as trellis for climbing plants. Try drilling a hole in your house wall, insert a rawlplug, plop in a masonry screw and then use this as a hook or a point to tie the plant frame on to. This works well for jasmine, passion fruit, vine and honeysuckle. Or cover the wooden sides with chicken wire and fix firmly beside a vegetable bed to use as a solid climber for peas, beans or cucumbers.

Hiring equipment

' Japanese homes are so small, so it is convenient to rent the things you use for only a short time, such as a baby bath or bassinet. It means we can send back the items as soon as we finish using them – I only needed the plastic bath for about two months. Of course in Japan, we have cheap baby items but many people feel it is *mottainai* if they throw something away. *Mottainai* has a unique Japanese sense, but it encourages us to cherish what we have now and make use of things as much as possible. It means that we should not produce a new thing, if we can share anything. Throwing away is out of question, recycling is better and reusing is the best.

Ryoko, 39, with Riki, ten, and Sumire, seven

It is possible to hire many items that you need only short term for your baby. You can find your nearest baby equipment rental business by searching Google. You should be able to find everything from strollers and stair gates, to monitors and mountain buggies to sterilisers and breast pumps. These companies provide good as new and reconditioned items, so it could be a good way to try out an expensive buggy or fix a crisis on holiday if something essential has been forgotten. Some hire firms will also assemble the flat-pack items that they provide. Below is a range of equipment that you can easily hire:

- **Super-duper electric breast pump** – NCT, www. nctpregnancyandbaby care.com
- **Baby car seats and booster seats (until approx. ten years)** – car hire company (ask when you book a car/taxi)
- **Bikes and bike trailers suitable for babies and young children** – bike shops on or near the 5,000 miles of Sustrans traffic-light and traffic-free cycle paths. See more at www.sustrans.org
- **Travel cot** – available at some hotels and YHAs (ideally book when you make a reservation), www.yha.org.uk
- **Kiddy wetsuits** – offered at surf shops and ideal for seaside and beach play, whatever the weather

For a deposit some shops let you try items out for set times, an hour maybe, sometimes longer. This is a great way to try out a bike or a buggy.

Clothes

> When you are about to have a baby just buy the basics, an all-in-one and a cardy because you'll be inundated by presents.
> Tara, 37, with Olivia, ten, Eve, seven, and Orla, four

From a very early age you can make your newborn look like a mini me in kidult chinos or dotty skirt, but clothing your baby need not be expensive, nor do they need everything brand spanking new. If you stick with the all-in-one uniform your child will look like a baby for longer, and you've got a day/ night combination that keeps draughts out, is easy to change and, as it is an all in one, will help keep those pesky cloth nappies in place. Wool tights and vests with poppers work well too, whatever the gender.

> I'd never bought second-hand clothes for myself, so I never thought about getting them for my baby – until I saw how fast he was growing. Now I use eBay for clothing, presents and equipment.
> Clare, 38, with Conor, three, and Finn, six months

Friends with older children, second-hand specialist children's shops and charity shops are all good sources of new-to-you clothing. Amongst new mums there is a real culture of swapping clothes, passing on items and chatting about what to get where, so it is very unlikely that you will feel stigmatised for buying anything second-hand. In fact, you may find people a little jealous of your good luck at spotting baby-sized bargains.

Ninety per cent of my kids clothes are second-hand, they come from friends, charity shops and, when I'm time-pressed, eBay. Being honest, I'd say they do look scruffier than everyone else's kids! I think this is a combination of using second-hand clothes and our washing system (we don't use a powder with artificial brighteners).

Hannah, 34, with Iola, three, and Cai, ten months

Tip

Worn out doesn't mean throw out

When your children really wear out their clothes don't throw them immediately into the bin. Really stained stuff can become rags for cleaning. Or cut into squares to make handkerchiefs, or bigger sizes to use as washable mealtime wipes. Or use for craft projects. If you feel embarrassed taking ripped trousers, stained shirts and saggy knickers to a charity shop, just label the bag as 'rags' and try handing that over. Many second-hand specialists, such as the Marie Curie chain, are able to make use of just about anything.

You can give special pieces to friends, or sell the best things on eBay. You may be lucky and live near a specialist second-hand clothes shops where you get a third of the sale price. Nurseries often need socks, trousers and tops and will gladly accept your outgrown items. What's left can go to charity shops or be bagged up and sold at the next NCT or car boot sale.

> I feel strongly about passing on clothes. It seems crazy not to. Over the past four years I've been sharing a common set of maternity wear and infant clothes with three colleagues. It's been a pleasure sharing. I really like knowing that my son Danny's clothes went to my colleagues' babies and now I'm using them again on my five-month-old, Thomas.
>
> Sandra, 42, with Danny, three, and Thomas, five months

Run your own swish

Despite the pictures of celebrity mums looking svelte a few days after they've given birth, most women take about nine months to regain their pre-pregnancy shape – so you may find that your urge to go clothes shopping stays on hold. It's a different story when you are pregnant as you will soon find some clothes just don't fit. If you haven't got a big jumper/ loose shirt and elasticated jeans you could try borrowing from a friend, or sharing with colleagues that you know have recently had a baby. It doesn't just save you cash, it can increase your friendship bonds too.

A fun way around the baby and your what-to-wear challenge is to get together with some friends and organise to swap clothes that you no longer wear/fit/want. Posh clothes swaps – known as a swish – are a growing trend and a lovely way to experiment with a new look without spending anything.

To run a swish, send out an invite (email or text will do) asking between eight to ten women to come over to your house on a set date for about two hours. They should bring with them between one and five items of clean and unspoiled clothing that they love but no longer wear – make sure that they know that this isn't a jumble! It helps to think of the clothes as vintage or pre-loved, rather than cast-offs. The point of a swish is to find a good home for those high-quality, well-maintained items that you'll never wear again and revitalise your wardrobe with some new-to-you items.

You could hold a swish after lunch so that some babies sleep in their buggies or pep up the event so the babies stay with a babysitter and your guests try on clothes with a glass of something nice and an eye on a full-length mirror. Another tip is to hang the items to give away on a rail to show off the selection of trousers/dresses and tops. You could also have a table for accessories. Any unwanted clothes can be taken back by whoever brought them, or you can collect them up and take to the nearest charity shop. Clothes swapping inspires storytelling. Everyone wants to talk about what they did in their clothes – and recipients love to hear the adventures of their new clothing.

> I've already worn the gold suit I picked out as fancy dress to a Purim party – complete with a white curly wig and pink shades. I intend to wear it as a serious piece of evening attire to a dinner party on Saturday, so will see how it goes down! I feel very proud having such a groovy hand-me-down.
>
> Penny, 38, with Netta, six, and Alma, three

How about adapting this idea and running a baby clothes swish? Just ask guests to bring a few items that are no longer worn by their child and a give-and-take mentality. You could

Tackling fast fashion

One mum who has set out to tackle the failings of fast fashion is the utterly stylish Dilys Williams, who has worked with two renowned eco-designers Katharine Hamnett (big on organic) and Stella McCartney (won't use leather or fur). Dilys heads the London College of Fashion's centre for sustainable fashion where she encourages tomorrow's designers to create new pieces fashioned from well-made, older garments. It's a modern tweak to the trend for vintage chic. 'Be proud of who you are and think about your identity – and make sure your clothes reflect that identity,' says Dilys.

'If we all loved our clothes more that would change the impact of the fashion industry dramatically. We don't have to be a martyr to ethical fashion and wear grungy items. But we will only get more choice if we go to the kind of designers and retailers that offer what we like.' So:

- Look for something that is your style.
- Demand more from retailers – such as Gap, Next, Monsoon, Top Shop and Primark – by asking how does this piece impact on the environment? How was it made? Who made it?
- It sounds radical, but don't wash your clothes as much. Instead care for them better and repair them.
- Reuse something you already have. Some designers take a material and then upscale it; maybe make it more beautiful or fit better.

ask one or two people at your event to take any of the unwanted items to a charity shop so you don't get left with extra bags of work. I've trialled this at my children's primary school and found it helped encourage people to see the cash and quality benefits of acquiring a pre-loved item. For anyone who really doesn't want to put their children into a used garment it also provides a new way of retiring outgrown clothes and shoes in an environmentally friendly way.

Sewing skills

Developing some basic mending skills is going to make clothes last longer, and helps pre-loved items fit better. Sewing can be satisfying and you will get better every time you have a go. Even if you do nothing else, sew on loose buttons before they fall off and get lost. If you are really skint or simply haven't time to look for the next sized all-in-one you can make it fit comfortably for a few more weeks by cutting off the outfit's toes, or the whole foot section from the heel. This is an emergency trick that can be used as your baby grows out of their shoes too. However, it does mean that the item is not so easy to pass on to another child and may have to go to the rag pile early.

If you already know how to sew and want to practise, try buying motifs or cutting them out of felt and stitch them on to an all-in-one or towel to make your child's clothes unique. It'll help you recognise your kit too if your baby goes to a childminder or nursery. It is even more efficient to use a specially bought marker pen to write your child's name on any clothes that need to be easily identified. Or suggest the nursery buys the pen, secure it with a length of twine and leave in the hallway or main reception area for shared use.

Tip

Sewing kit

Make a sewing kit by storing a packet of needles, sharp scissors, reel of dark and light cotton and a packet of pins. You could also try saving loose buttons in a jar and collecting together some material scraps to use when you need to deal with a lost button, patch knees or fix a tear.

Storing and labelling

Great ways to create space-saving, moth-proof storage include suitcases, zipped laundry bags and vacuum-pack plastic bags. Make sure you label the items carefully and wash and neatly fold the clothes before you store them. That way they can be passed on to your next child or a friend with no embarrassment, they are less likely to become moth maternity wards and you could sell them on eBay.

' I wouldn't wear second-hand clothes so it would be hypocritical to make my children wear used clothes. But I don't throw clothes away, I keep them for cousins in Bangladesh or donate them to people in poorer countries through the mosque. I'd never give someone I know in the UK clothes my children had worn. I wouldn't buy something new, either: if you had a baby you might not like my taste so I'd give you money so you could buy things you needed. '
Sultana, 24, with Omar, six, and Jarah, four

If you are unwilling to pass on your children's outgrown clothes to people you know, use bins put aside by councils for recycling clothes, which provide anonymous distribution to good causes.

Feel-good ethical shopping

In an ideal world I'd source everything from Britain, but where would you go and do that? So much is made in China. I want things that are well made and last a long time. There's nothing wrong with conserving things or repairing them. With furniture, we got a change table that will transform itself into a desk. The cot turns into a sofa, two chairs, and a bed that can be used until he's eight years old. They weren't cheap but they don't break and I like the idea of reusing these things.
Anne, 43, with Edgar, five months

Over the past 20 years ethical businesses have been springing up like cowslips on motorway verges, many run by 'mumpreneurs' who have decided to invest in products they felt passionate about. The range of businesses mums run is staggering, from eco-party products to sew-your-own clothes kits. Some have sprung up to address a need: Green People, www.greenpeople.co.uk, which sells organic skin and hair care products for all the family, was founded by Charlotte Vohtz trying to find something that would ease her two-year-old daughter's eczema.

Just because a company is run by a mum doesn't mean the claims for their products can be accepted without question.

Organisations such as Ethical Consumer and Ethical Junction help consumers compare credentials, though like, *Which?*, both require you to be a member, see www.ethicalconsumer.org and www.ethical-junction.org. You can also find products independently certified as being from sustainable woodlands; organic; fair-traded; vegan; biodynamic, etc., by going to the home organisation's website and checking out what's available near you.

A tiny selection of green favourites include Green Baby, People Tree, the Welsh sports/outdoor gear from Howies, and the Natural Collection, which was winner of the Best Online Retailer in the *Observer*'s Ethical Awards in 2006, 2007 and 2008. Shopping at these eco-specialists has a proper feel-good factor, as Al Tepper from the Natural Collection explains: 'Consumer support for sustainable innovation and ethical products can bring massive change to our world and benefit the future of our children.' Tepper is convinced that buying ethical products or from an ethical business gives more mainstream manufacturers the incentive to try out ecological and fair-trade sourcing, which is a win-win for us all.

In fact, many high-street stockists provide a limited range of fair-trade and organic goods in their stores. You are still likely to pay more, especially if you are buying clothes, but parting with a few extra pounds can give you the satisfaction of knowing what you've bought is giving a fair living wage to suppliers so they are able to feed, educate and deal with the health emergencies of their own families.

Baby steps

Small

○ Choose well-made, quality products that last.

○ Sew on that loose button before you lose it – a two-minute job that will keep your coat or blouse looking good, not tatty.

Medium

○ Bookmark and join your nearest Freecycle group; also eBay, Gumtree and any other swap/network sites.

○ Make regular visits to the charity shops (inc. specialist clothes groups, like Traid and Oxfam vintage), ask friends/family if they've got outgrown clothes to give away. Aim to always look for second-hand before buying new – gradually, the thrill of finding something you want for less than it would be new adds to the pleasure of the chase.

○ Join the library for books, DVDs and music. Or just ask friends if you can borrow favourites. Get a wanted/for sale list going at places mums and babies regularly meet.

Large

○ Take a lesson from the downshifters: cut your costs – the more you spend, the more you need to earn. Set yourself a challenge: could you buy nothing for a month (except essentials)?

○ Join your nearest NCT or Transition Town (or neighbourhood) group to see if you can start to pool baby items that aren't needed for long or are only needed for a particular season.

Three
Gifts and Celebrations

Here are some tried and tested ways to create unique and useful presents with even very little children. If nothing else, it sets up a make-it-yourself precedent that will put off the day you'll need to dish out pocket money. However, other people will certainly want to give your children presents, so here's some advice on limiting the amount that you receive. Giving the gift of time is so much more precious for a child than a toy that has no story behind it and is easily broken or discarded.

Gifts to Give – or Create with – Your Child

Leo's granny bought him an apple tree for his first birthday, and he loves the little apples. He'll be able to watch it grow as he gets older.
Rita, 38, with Leo, two, and Rosa, seven months

As little ones have no purse power, it's a real opportunity to use their artistic skills and playfulness to create personalised gifts. For the little boy with his own fruit tree this might be as loving as picking an apple and offering it to Granny, or as simple as helping mum turn apples into delectable treats like pie, crumble or chutney to be given as a birthday gift.

If staying up late to sew a special present – a buffalo-decorated teepee that will fit your living room, or embroidering your baby's name on a bedspread – gives you satisfaction then definitely do it. But another way of creating play things, gifts and lengthen childhood memories is to make things with your child.

Make a scrapbook

It's lovely to make keepsakes about your child's babyhood that could be a talking point forever. An album of digital photos and short videos are one way (just make sure you back it up) but when your children are older and ask you to recall their first birthday, it's easier for them to have something physical to hold, like a scrapbook.

It can be fun to help your child enjoy seeing the passing of the seasons or remember holiday adventures by creating an occasional diary where you stick in their own artwork, handprints, party invites, dried flowers, sweet wrappers, etc., as well as photos. Either keep up the habit as a book of annual achievements (later it can be a record of the victories of growing up – nursery graduation, assembly certificates, learning to swim) or plan it as a gift with themes that the recipient will enjoy.

‘What I'd like to do is put together a nature diary, an old-fashioned thing where the baby and I do a bit of drawing or we might look at different types of leaves or take some photos through the seasons and enjoy looking at them now and when he's older. ’

Anne, 43, with Edgar, six months

Dressing-up kit

Children adore dressing up. So get a dressing-up box together and include such things as frothy dresses, tiaras, wigs, hats, ribbons, clickety-clack shoes, moustaches, big ears, Comic Relief noses and pirate gear. Whatever you add will give an extra frisson to the children's games and may inspire amateur dramatics.

Den-making kit

I gave my three-year-old a large lidded box filled with lengths of material, clothes pegs, net curtains, hooks, thin rope, some very basic tools and a deer antler, and told her it was a den-making kit. On reflection, she may have been a little young for it, but using it together, the whole family has had a lot of fun. It makes setting up a den in a room or garden simple, and keeps all the equipment in one easy-to-locate place.

Edible gifts

Once your child can sit up, you can start creating tasty gifts, some of which might be suitable for giving away. Try adding a vanilla pod or a big scoop of cinnamon to make flavoured sugar. Your child should decorate the label (just press on a sticky envelope label or cut out something designed on a PC and fix with a dab of glue). Little children can also help make chocolate truffles, paint hard-boiled eggs and decorate fairy cakes. Supermarkets and specialist cooking shops and websites have incredible decorating choices, although icing sugar and chocolate buttons are good corner shop standbys when decoration is essential.

Edible gifts keep better in air-tight containers so collect up unwanted biscuit tins during the year, ready for the present-giving season. Improve a scratched tin by letting your toddler cover it with one of their masterpieces (cover with sticky back plastic for longer life). Or posh up with stickers or decoupage or decorate by gluing on beach combings.

Make you own flapjacks

If you are against the clock, flapjacks are a winner. They take 40 minutes from start to finish and are easy for little children to stir. They can be made incredibly sweet and gooey or extra healthy to suit whoever you wish to give it to.

230g porridge oats	**Options:**
150g brown sugar	cinnamon
150g butter	pumpkin seeds
	raisins/sultanas

- ○ Grease a baking tin approximately 21 x 21 cm.
- ○ Melt butter in a big saucepan over low heat, add sugar and stir until sauce-like.
- ○ Remove from heat and stir in oats. (Now's the time to shake in cinnamon or add a handful of pumpkin seeds or raisins/sultanas.)
- ○ Transfer to the greased tin press, down hard with back of a spoon.
- ○ Put in oven to cook at 180°C/350°F/gas mark 4.
- ○ After about 30 minutes, when the flapjacks look golden brown, remove from oven and immediately cut into 12 or 16 pieces, but leave put so they cool in the tin.

○ When cold, remove from the tin. Add any broken pieces to your muesli as if they were granola. Keeps well, but too tasty to resist.

Chocolate krispies can be a lovely vegan treat – just mix cornflakes and melted plain chocolate and allow to cool.

Fairy feeding stations

Children have a close relationship to fairies – they love hearing the stories, dressing in wings and are attracted to littleness, so creating a special fairy place is a logical bit of play. It may also help you teach colours and names of plants as your child finds fallen petals/catkins/leaves that they think the fairies might like as a duvet, dog bed, hospital or throne...

For more ideas about using fairies and wizards to entertain and learn about the magic of wildflowers and woodlands (and how to make a wand), see the Fairyland Trust info and family days out at www.fairyland.org.

I'm a high priestess of wicca and my tradition focuses on nature and honouring Gaia, so my two children were raised in the States, hiking, camping, saving prairie dogs before developers rolled in, etc., etc. You'll see that children love to build little nature shrines and you can make any kind of little place in your back garden for honouring or cherishing something. Say you had a little flower garden and want to honour the fairy folk so you can grow more flowers and vegetables. As a naturalist, I'd look at how you fix nitrogen in the soil and the best ways of composting and gardening organically, but at the same time it is very important to thank the devas or fairies.

Fran Howell, 51, wildlife campaigner and author of *Making Magic with Gaia* **(Red Wheel/Weiser, 2002)**

Mini worlds

Make these in a sandpit or, for a portable option, use a shoe/cereal box. Inside create a miniature garden using a heap of soil (or compost), petals, a scrap of silver foil (or mirror) for a pond, twigs and stones. You and your child could draw and cut out your own scary monsters/dinosaurs, prince/princesses, goblins/giants to help establish the mood of his very own world.

Passed-on and pre-loved gifts

If you can steel yourself to share something you or your now older children once loved try passing it on to a child of the right age and gender to enjoy it. This could be a football club pillowcase, a favourite soft toy patched and repaired, or a set of wooden alphabet blocks, perhaps freshly painted, or an outgrown scooter. Or it could be books you've loved, such as Lauren Child's wonderful series – toddlers love someone reading to them from *I Am too Absolutely Small for School* and *I Will Not Ever Never Eat a Tomato*.

Portraits and pictures

Collecting up your baby's scribbly and spider-like self-portraits is fascinating. You can store in a large art folder, or other dedicated space, and then pull out for a special family show. Or you can use the heaps of artwork as wrapping paper for other gifts. Try providing thick crayons that are easier for your children to hold. Water-based paint is always fun to use because the results are instant and dramatic. Children can paint sitting at a table but it is often easier if you pin a large sheet on to an easel with a bulldog clip, get your child into an apron and then let them create masterpieces with as much mess as they like.

' Our front room has a wall dedicated to artwork done by Finn and his cousins, whom we insist do a new picture when they come to visit and I'm forever doing pictures of someone or something that Finn likes, be it Charlie and Lola or the local cat. As well as the wall, we also have a drawing easel permanently out in the front room which means that it gets a lot of use and most visitors are now encouraged by Finn to draw something when they're here. Long may the messiness and creativity continue! '

Elaine, 44, with Finn, two, and Niall, two weeks

Wildlife care

Watching birds on a feeding station you made and regularly stock with peanuts, bird seeds, or any other wildlife is fascinating for young children, even those who have a pet at home anyway. As your child gets older you can help her learn more about the natural world by leaving out books or directing her to relevant websites (the Field Study Centre is the oracle – see the Resources section for details).

○ **Bird table** – you can buy or make a conventional bird table, or position a trunk stump outside a window. Ideally, keep it away from bushes and shrubs to stop cats disturbing/picking off your birds. Fit hooks on the underside so you can hang up nuts, fat balls or coconuts filled with seed mix.

○ **Bird feeders** – find a pine cone on a walk, hook some wire or string around the top and then coat in a mix of lard, peanut butter and tasty seeds. You can fill small yoghurt tubs (make a hole at the top through which you string a hoop) with this mix, but the pine cone solution is much more elegant when emptied by the birds. Find useful ideas at the youth/make-do page at The Royal Society for the Protection of Birds: www.rspb.org.uk.

○ **Bumblebees** – watch your bumblebees bumbling and how they tumble into flowers with deep cups. You can encourage nesting sites by leaving an area of your garden quite wild. In a low sheltered spot place an old bird box, three bricks with a slate on the top, watering can on its side, etc., and perhaps stuff with some moss or a little bit of straw (borrow from a friend with a rabbit/guinea pig, etc.).

○ **Wildflowers** – sowing a wildflower mix is the easiest way to guerrilla garden with young children, but don't let them shake out a whole pack – instead, get them crouching down and then drop a few teenie seeds on their hands and encourage them to blow them on to the ground. You should soon be able to identify cornflowers, poppies, camomile, pineapple weed – match up what you see with books.

○ **Mini beast area** – lay down a small piece of old carpet, bit of thick cardboard, a heap of bricks or logs a parent could lift up at an angle so you can enjoy looking at wood lice (slaters) or centipedes with so many legs that you've just got to have a go counting them. As children get older a magnifying glass or bug viewer offers a new view of well-known insects such as ants, shield bugs and ladybirds. If you can supervise children safely and have permission you could also try pond dipping. Take a pale-coloured bucket or washing-up bowl, scoop out some pond water, wait for any silt to settle, then check what pond life you've have got using an ID guide. Later return everything to the pond.

○ **Beautiful plant books** – these can help children play wildlife I-Spy. Try *A Little Guide to Wild Flowers* and a *Little Guide to Trees* published by the Eden Project. These are created by stunning children's illustrator Charlotte Voake (you may already know her style if you've read *Ginger* and *Here Comes the Train*).

If you can fence off a pond (with a high latched or more secure gate) or cover it with a child-proof grille then a pond would be a wonderful present for a child and give years of pleasure and opportunity for scientific study. Once taught to catch newts without harming them, newts often joined playtime in the dolls' house my four-year-old daughter kept outside.

Spring a surprise

Try wrapping up a cucumber or pineapple and see what pleasure level a pre-schooler gets from it. It's the wrapping paper that babies love, especially their first few Christmases.

Safe and tidy

Firm favourites may be kept for a lifetime, but as children grow up you will probably need to bag outgrown items (or not yet age appropriate) and store. Ideally, mark clearly for future use or pass on to share with friends, or swap in a toy exchange.

Losing a beloved toy can be heartbreaking for your child, and costly or next-to-impossible for you to replace. It's also embarrassing retracing your route asking every person if they've seen your child's special fluffy toy. A simple solution is to sew a long ribbon on to the toy so you can tie it to your buggy or baby backpack (be alert to the dangers of strangulation from a long cord). At nursery you could write your child's name on it with a permanent marker pen or sew a name tag to his toy.

Toy repair kit

For injured toys repair can include a good wash with basic washing-up liquid (for indoor toys left outdoors), treatment with the correct glue, deft use of rubber bands (found on many postal delivery walking routes) and access to a sewing kit (new buttons, booster stuffing, etc.). For more sophisticated repairs search the web for toy hospitals.

Gift Limitations

People love to give babies presents. All manner of friends and acquaintances will knit, sew, draw and send your baby outfits, football-themed slippers and patterned bibs. Far too many people also gift plastic toys that soon clutter your rooms and fuel the environmental pollution in China, where they are made.

> I love to give anything wooden or books. I sometimes buy second-hand all-in-ones and decorate them with fabric pens, usually black spots (think Dalmatian) and once we did make a set of wooden blocks by chopping up and sanding random bits of scrap wood. It was lots of work, though.
>
> Caroline, 33, with Madeleine, six, and Rudy, four

If you're trying to be greener, then you should avoid any toys that break easily or have a limited enjoyment factor. Unfortunately, many people associate generosity with spending money. Try to steer friends and family away from trinkets that can be easily picked up in a shop to gifts that have a story behind them. Unusual presents that little children love and cannot be found in the shops include old glasses cases that snap shut, Granny's old teddy, costume jewellery, a giant cardboard box which can be turned into a house, car, den, dinosaur or whatever your child's imagination wants it to be. Ideally, get the gift-giver to take time to decorate it with your child using paints/wax crayons and letting them do the main design work. Children also love ball pools – make your own with a box and tennis balls.

> There's great present recycling on eBay. Emile's Christmas present was two massive bundles of fancy-dress clothes, one of the lots was only 99p! They were all stuffed into a pirate treasure chest that my mum found in a junk shop. Emile was ecstatic. Also his last

birthday present was about £100's worth of second-hand Lego from eBay for £15.

Becky, 37 with Emile, four, and Celeste, five months

Tip

Toy libraries can help you find out if your child loves a toy or just wants to enjoy it for a brief play date – use it like a conventional library. One innovative toy library in Muswell Hill, London, sells gift tokens to pay for a year's membership for an under-eight-year-old. As there are 800 toys to choose from, this is a practical way to enable grandparents to find exactly the right present.

I'm slightly dreading Christmas. Conor's third birthday coincided with big brother presents [given to Conor when the baby was born] and so much stuff came into the house. We were wondering whether to say, can you get him presents which we know he's interested in – Lego and model cars – but we don't want to question people's judgement. I wonder too what Finn will ever get as a present. Even his baby gym used to be Conor's.

Clare, 38, with Conor, three, and Finn, six months

Gifts pile up at certain times of the year, but another difficulty can be trying to find ways to stop generous family members buying more than one present each celebration, or even bringing little gifts every time they visit. Try reminding you-know-who that your home is small and extra possessions can only really fit in if something already loved and treasured gets given away – something most small children find tear-fully tough.

'The main culprit for wanting to give more than one present to each child is my mother-in-law so my husband has a quiet word before every visit, birthday and at Christmas time. He has explained that we are trying to be less materialistic and make each present important and valuable rather than one of dozens. It's been quite painful getting her to understand that giving lots of presents devalues each one. We also explain that it's not fair on the other granny if she gives the children more. '
Jo, 39, with Ben, five, and Sally, two

If you think clarifying your home's present policy is a lost cause ask for practical gifts such as pants, socks, PJs, swimming kit, beach shoes, slippers, wellies or equipment such as a bike seat or buggy board.

Shared memories = ideal gifts

○ Books. It's lovely to get a title that used to be a favourite of the giver when they were small. You can always pick out a library copy first to see which goes down better – Judith Kerr's *Mog* or *The Tiger who Came to Tea* or Shirley Hughes's *Dogger*. Remind yourself that 'small is beautiful' when buying books for kids, you really don't need to buy every story in a series. Instead, let the child work up an appetite for their favourite. That way if they get given a book token they will know what book they want to own next.

○ Puppets (ready-made or make together), plus a gift of time to help develop stories, stage sets and props. Even very little children love to put on a show.

○ Rocking horse, outdoor rocker, sandpit, swing, musical instrument, no-pedal bike, scooter. These big gifts can be used for a long time.

○ Doll's house furniture, den-making/doctor's kit, and found objects. Help children fantasy-play.

○ Pocket money for collectibles or second-hand CDs, tapes, DVDs to be bought when seen at car boot sales

○ Personal selection of bath toys (ideally, floaters and sinkers)

○ Gifts that encourage creative skills or that you need, e.g., clothes, shoes, plants/small fruit trees, garden toys. Or vouchers for something to look forward to, e.g., a trip to a farm or a zoo, etc. Or suggest suppliers that you like.

Asking for cash

A survey by PayPal, which specialises in online transactions, found that UK shoppers spend £8 billion on Christmas presents each year, yet more than £78 million will be returned to the shops in the new year because they just weren't what the receiver wanted. You can suggest presents or ask for givers to restrict their purchases to pre-loved items, but your requests may be ignored unless you specify a really simple option: money.

Asking for cash does seem an unexpected demand by families trying to green their lives – supposedly by trying to limit their consumer purchases – but money is the only thing that enables parents to buy exactly what they want, at the time they (or their child) needs it. Your generous friend or family member could add to your child's tax-free account or top up her Child Trust Fund, the government attempt to encourage families with newborns to start saving for their children by giving them a £250 voucher to keep in a savings fund that can only be accessed when she turns 18.

> My friends wanted to give a present to the baby so I sent a really gentle email early in December saying that we didn't want anything, but if they wanted to give a present then second-hand was not a problem. Handmade gifts are lovely, or they could put money into an account for when she's older.
>
> **Holly, with River, seven months**

Toys Not 4 Us

Recent stories about poor health and safety practices in Chinese factories have seen well-known toy brands withdrawn; in 2007 around 21 million were recalled. Some of these are sure to end up in second-hand shops or car boot sales so make it a family rule that no toys – especially plastic or small model figures – should be chewed. This is very hard when toddlers are teething so if they are in chewy mood just remove the toy and distract them. If you have doubts about the provenance of some toys then make sure to wash your child's hands after playing and before eating. That way they don't suck fingers and take in an unwelcome dose of lead paint, VOCs or any other nasty picked up from the floor or toy.

Celebrations

Celebrating a birth

Giving birth is such a huge event in itself, just having a happy, healthy new baby is celebration enough. But once you recover it's lovely to celebrate the arrival of a new person in the world with friends and family. Below are some ideas about ways people prepare for and celebrate the arrival of a new baby.

Blessingways

An antidote to baby showers. At a blessingway the expectant mum-to-be invites female relatives and friends (and possibly midwife, doula or other birthing assistant) to a party to give her confidence for giving birth. The idea is borrowed from a Native American tradition where women bring or send a bead to make a necklace that the expecting mum will wear during labour. But you could create something together instead, such as a wildflower patch, a quilt or a piece of art. More practically, the woman's best friends and close relatives could organise a rota system for dropping by, tidying up, minding any other children or cooking a meal to help the new mum recover and focus on her little baby. Find out more at www.naturalbirthandbabycare.com.

Thanking God

Christenings, where several close friends/family promise to be godparents and look after your child's spiritual welfare as he or she is dedicated to God, are traditionally held within three months of your child's birth (although they may be many months later); while circumcision of boys is generally done within days of their birth.

Muslims share the name of their children after sacrificing an animal to celebrate the arrival of a new baby, a ceremony known as Aqueeqah. The goat (or cow) gets shared out with the poor, making a baby's arrival a very happy communal event that happens seven days after the birth. There will also be a party for family and friends at which the baby's hair may be shorn and, when weighed, the amount matched with a gift in gold or the cash equivalent to charity.

Other ways

There are the old religions to look at, there's the Humanist (no religion) option, see www.humanism.org.uk, with its naming ceremonies and opportunity for guide parents) and there's the DIY freestyle – all should include focus, thanks and a bit of feasting.

If you are following your own spiritual instincts you may find that the pleasures and possibilities of dreaming up how to welcome your child, and giving thanks for their safety, takes time. Rather than having 'godparents', you may choose to have 'oddparents', especially good if you or your friends are atheist or agnostic.

Tip

Some families bury the placenta in a special place, under or near a fruit tree. Others flambé the placenta following Hugh Fearnley-Whittingstall's instructions and make it into a pâté for the new parents to enjoy.

Birthday parties

I offer to take along vegan versions of party food.
I actually see this as a bonus as it means I can do
"party" food and keep it healthy. I have always
explained to Saffron why we choose a vegan diet.
If ever she misses out on a treat at school or a club
then I make it up to her with a special treat later –
she knows this and so doesn't get upset or feel
like she's missing out.

Sharon, 40, with Saffron, nine

We have huge parties with 30–40 kids in a hall. Rather
than party bags, I hand out second-hand books – each
is a repeat of one of my kid's favourites and wrapped
in newspaper. I collect them through the year from the
local library chuck-out pile or from car boots.

Zoe, 39, with Mati, six, and Pip, three

Tip

Keeping down the invite list

Just invite over the same number of friends as your child's new
age. So a one-year-old gets one friend. Next year you could invite
two friends for your two-year-old – who may well come with a
carer and sibling so the numbers soon swell. Keeping the same
number of guests as your child's age pays off big time when your
11-year-old asks for a birthday disco for 30 classmates…

While children are small, simple food and old-fashioned games are what they want. Popular games to play include:

○ Pass the parcel (tip: don't start putting a present between every layer and don't always let the birthday child win this, as children lose interest if they think they haven't a chance)
○ Pin the tail on the donkey
○ Musical statues
○ Treasure hunt
○ Clean up shaving-foam-covered model farm animals
○ Racing team games
○ Leave time for throwing wrapping paper around the room (and then folding it up for reuse) and plenty of free play

The party bag debate

'It's easy to make your own party bags, and then the bag is the gift. I found some fair-trade Indian organic cotton and then made drawstring bags with bits of old ribbon. On each bag I embroidered the initial of the guest's first name. I did it in the evenings when I was watching the news on TV. Everyone was so thrilled. '
Julie, 45, with Freya, 10, and Clara, seven

'Party bags for two-year-olds? Under NO circumstances! '
Laurie, 44, with Maise, 11, and Finlay, two

Not giving party bags is fine. No little child – except a few pre-schoolers with older siblings – expects them. But for lots of children a party bag is a lovely going-home treat that makes leaving the exciting party a little easier. And for green parents making a party bag can be a chance to show off all the creative things you can do. Besides drawn/painted cards, try decorating used horseshoes, rocks, rosettes, badges or press bird seed feeders on to a pine cone. If inspiration is failing, simply use acrylic paints to create a pattern and the child's name or favourite animal on to a bit of wood or even a drinking glass. A creative alternative is to make or decorate something with the guests at the party which can then be taken home. Easy to organise ideas include decorating biscuits/cupcakes or painting a tile (often available on Freecycle), making a coil pot or planting some seeds/bulbs.

More gifts of time

Of course, it's not just children who love presents, adults love giving and receiving gifts too. Offer priceless promises for close friends (a massage, an hour of gardening, free time hours while you babysit their children) instead of gifts with a price tag. For a new parent the best present is to bring round a dish of food to eat now or pop in the freezer – this sort of practical support makes being a new mum much easier, whether they are on their first or fifth baby. Or you could take a bag of useful shopping (bread, tea bags, organic milk) and make the new mum a cuppa. Don't leave without sorting out the washing-up, either.

Make an effort to prevent important days disappearing just because you are busy adjusting to parenthood. If you can't get a babysitter, or don't want to, just take the baby too and go out and enjoy a special day. Even if it's raining hard you can have fun looking around an art gallery, sheltering in a ruin or popping into a pub you always meant to try. Indoor or outdoor picnics can be a cheap and happy way to mark significant dates. A simple to organise party, with minimal time taken clearing up, is an enviably easy way to create a happy celebration.

Baby steps

Small

○ Gather together art materials so that children can make their own greeting cards (hand- and footprints are a great design, especially if your child is too small/unable to scribble).

○ Save paper bags to use as party bags (you can always decorate them).

○ Ask friends and family to get presents for you from a present list or donate cash towards something you want for your child, or put money in an account until your child needs it.

Medium

○ Get creative and stop spending money on cards and gifts. Think up what your friend or family love and then try and make that happen.

○ Gifts of time are invaluable so suggest that your family member spends time with your children rather than giving them another toy.

○ Let your baby learn by getting them involved in your life rather than blitzing them with toys marketed as learning aids. So-called 'educational toys' may be salve to you, but any self-respecting toddler is going to prefer having a go at what you are doing rather than being put into a pen with a plastic collection of educational toys. If you want to try the Baby Mozart experience you can always borrow from a friend or the nearest toy library.

○ If you can't produce something on a birthday then create a voucher saying you will be looking for just the right-sized one. This allows an older child to be involved in the hunt for a special present.

○ Organise a proper picnic kit, including water containers, rug, etc.

○ Offer to leaflet nearby homes with details about your nearest toy library.

Large

○ Set up a toy library, or just do swaps with families with similarly aged children.

○ Plan a really green party. Film a bit to relive it in the future.

Four
Food – What's Your Child Eating?

What you offer for dinner is an unexpectedly simple way to keep your family from battering Mother Earth.

The most basic survival skill you can teach your child is how to eat healthily, which will ensure that they can choose, cook and grow the right stuff. Ideally, you start this by giving your child a long start on breast milk. But even if the breastfeeding went painfully wrong, you can still provide really good, early food lessons by helping your toddler to identify all sorts of foods at shops and supermarkets. Go to a farmers' market and enjoy looking at the heaped piles of fruit and veg. Do taste tests: slice up two apples and see which tastes sweeter, nicer, redder? The more curious you are about good eating, dealing with waste and finding meals that suit your budget, the more your child will learn. Cooking can be relaxing, creative and a lifesaver.

' Food is well tricky. I constantly have internal battles about wanting my children to have a varied and healthy diet while being aware that the season for many fruit and veg is actually quite short and the rest of the time they are being air-freighted from other countries. I freeze berries in the summer and then chuck them in smoothies. I also make homemade ice lollies out of smoothie mixture. Able and Cole do a weaning bag and don't air-freight.

Caroline, 33, with Madeleine, 6, and Rudy, 4

So what is good food? *New York Times* best-selling food writer Michael Pollen's great advice is to 'eat food, not too much, mostly vegetables'. He clearly wasn't feeding a toddler, who may switch from happily eating green mush and cherry tomatoes to outright refusal overnight. It's so unfair: we want to raise our kids healthy but they won't eat up their broccoli florets. The answer is to use tricks: challenge your toddler to eat up their peas using a fork, or their fingers, or with their eyes closed, or with chop sticks. Try puréeing into a sauce or add some carrots and celery as a tomato sauce base for spaghetti.

Learning to cook is best done watching, tasting and joining in. By cooking up some meals for your family and getting your toddler to stir a mix, or wipe the table (you can finish off the bits they miss), or find a saucepan, big wooden spoon or the olive oil, you will be subtly teaching your child to cook. You may find you get better at multi-tasking in the kitchen, especially if you stock up on plastic containers and a hand blender to create home-blended purées, soups and stews which can then be stored in mini portion sizes in an ice-cube tray.

Encourage kitchen craft by playing imaginary games like shopkeepers or running a café. A two-year-old with good concentration may be able to lay the table ready for a meal, get out the butter and tomato sauce or even pick some raspberries. Dress them up as super-hero waiters if that makes the task more fun for them.

‘ While my husband Gordon was down at the local tip he found a children's plastic play oven so now Finn spends a lot of time cooking on his oven and not only has it encouraged his creative play, but it's been interesting to hear what his top foods are (pasta and olives feature a lot). He's also discovered that he can help himself to the various jars of nuts and pulses within reach in a lower cupboard in the kitchen and, having discovered what is and isn't edible, now has a selection of mixed seeds and nuts down to a fine art. We've built on this by making mixed seed and nut flapjacks together and he also helps out with putting the toppings on pizzas and making mixed salads so I think cooking is going to be a fun and educative family pastime. ’

Elaine, 44, with Finn, two, and Niall, two weeks

You can also be canny about gardening by asking the places where you take your baby to play, such as drop-ins and nurseries, if they can plant up containers or manage a small vegetable garden. That way you and your children get to enjoy seeing and tasting plants without having the daily watering chore of a garden (which is made much greener if you install water butts at the same time).

‘ I buy grapes because they're healthy and one of the few things that Anna will readily eat. But, quite often, they are air-freighted – which I know is bad for the environment. I'm not proud of doing so – but I think it's impossible to do everything "right" – everyone has something that's difficult with their child. With

Anna, it's food. Just because I can't do everything in an eco way, doesn't mean that it's not worth doing something.

Sally, 38, with Anna, two

Parents are champion food worriers. For anyone up to speed on food there can be debates about what's best to buy, with the classics for eco eaters being local versus organic, fair trade versus air miles or more pragmatically, packaged versus home-made. However, even if you admit to being rather a food evangelist it pays off not to be too dogmatic. That's because if you boast that the only food that has passed your toddler's lips is organic this or homemade that you will soon alienate lots of friendly families who might have enjoyed play dates, childcare swaps and have been brilliant members of a babysitting circle. All of us parents are just doing our best, and there are many reasons why some people cannot take so much time or money sourcing or preparing their food.

Where I live it's important to let children have friends as locally as possible and not say, "No, you can't eat the junkie stuff at Brownies" or "No, you can't play with so-and-so because you might be served chicken nuggets." I'm not focusing anymore on the idea of green, just trying to help my kids be open to lots of different communities and people.

Annie, 45, with Elsa, seven, and Ned, five

Breastfeeding

Like everything to do with being a parent, don't beat yourself up if you can't do it perfectly.
Hannah, 34, Iola, three, and Cai, 10 months

Breast milk is free, instantly available and generates zero waste. However, breastfeeding is a skill, which both mum and baby need to learn. Although you need no extra calories to breast-feed, it is tiring and time-consuming in the first weeks of your baby's life (not to mention, rather painful). But as you start to measure your baby's age in months, breastfeeding is the easy, greenest option. It stops hurting, subtly helps you regain your figure and, unlike bottlefeeding, can be done on the go with no preparation. Its only drawback is that it is down to mum alone.

Your breast milk is perfectly suited for your child's age and provides your baby with some immunisation against all sorts of viruses and diseases, even after you've stopped doing it. And you don't have to sterilise anything. Because I breastfed my girls until they were 14 months they never needed a dummy or a bottle so they missed having to do the cold turkey that many toddlers are expected to endure when their families decide they need to give up their babyhood comforters.

The World Health Organization (WHO) recommends that babies should be breastfed for two years, but in the UK a child getting breast milk for longer than a year is lucky. This may be because we rarely see women breastfeeding in public, and those that do often have to put up with unexpected reac-tions from strangers and relations. To avoid an upsetting situation when breastfeeding is newish, or if your child is a breastfeeding toddler, take the easy option and feed in out-of-the-way spots – although don't let yourself be forced into a toilet. After all, who willingly eats dinner in a loo?

> Grannies of all persuasion have not been particularly supportive about breastfeeding. My parents required that Zoë feed in another room! All our parents are quite distant and elderly and non-involved. I think there is something to be said for the response that if they want to have a say over what is going on then they should do some of the work. But if they are sniping from afar, well, let them hang.
> Hugh, 42, dad of Mati, six, and Pip, three

'Women who breastfeed for longer have a lower risk of heart attacks, strokes and cardiovascular disease,' says Rosie Dodds from the National Childbirth Trust. There is also evidence that breastfeeding helps mums lose any weight gained during pregnancy, protects from breast and ovarian cancer and can help give mums stronger bones in later life. As the benefits stack up there has been a much needed cultural shift. When mum of four (and many other things) Paula Yates breastfed a walking, talking Tiger Lily in Oz the paparazzi lashed out. Nearly ten years later, in 2009, when actress Salma Hayek, who had a one-year-old, breastfed another woman's child on a UN visit to Sierra Leone (which has the highest infant mortality rate in the world) the media were sympathetic. Salma revealed how her great-grandmother did the same in Mexico long ago for a stranger's starving baby. The clip generated millions of YouTube hits and helped more people learn that WHO advice is to breastfeed exclusively for six months and then offered, along with solids, up to two years and beyond.

Breast milk may be a superfood but for extended breast-feeding – anything over a year – mums often get confusing advice because health officials rarely factor in that an older breastfed child consumes the same calories in two minutes as a newborn used to get from a 20-minute feed. As a result toddlers still having breast milk may also eat smaller amounts of solid food compared to fully weaned babies still on formula. And breastfed babies in the first weeks gain weight in a different, slower pattern than those pesky weighing-in charts demand. If you are ever confused about whether you are doing it right, feeding enough or too much, telephone the experts at NCT or La Leche League.

Tips for extended breastfeeding

- If you plan to breastfeed for months rather than weeks then from an early age refer to your milk as mummy's milk or num nums or use another language (lait, leche, susu) to prevent embarrassment when your inhibition-free toddler starts demanding tit or booby.
- Toddlers like to fiddle. If that usually means stroking your hair or your other breast you can distract them with a toy or nursing bead necklace.
- People will question why you haven't weaned your child yet. Prepare an answer, and mug up on the facts of life. Extended breastfeeding doesn't lessen the likelihood of becoming pregnant. Tandem breastfeeding doesn't deprive the baby.
- Stopping breastfeeding is your decision alone, but if your partner or office has a time limit of tolerance it is fine to wean your baby. You've done a great job.

Although it is a new research area breastfeeding mums are unknowingly doing that bit more to tackle climate change. In Gabrielle Palmer's *The Politics of Breastfeeding*, an important book which every parent should read, Palmer compares the carbon footprint of a carton of orange juice (though it could just as easily be formula) which emits 1.7kg of carbon dioxide. 'The bulk of this comes from production costs such as fertiliser, transport and fuel. In contrast a woman can produce hundreds of litres of super-fluid breast milk for a zero-carbon footprint.'

Expressing milk

'Back then I was the only person I knew who used a glass milk bottle. It didn't break. I'm pleased I used it as there's more and more information about plastics leaching.'
Tara, 37, with Olivia, ten, Eve, seven, and Orla, four

Expressing milk can be useful because it gives mum some time away from her baby, and allows the other parent, friend or carer to do the feeding. If you want to express milk (which can be done by hand or pump) or are bottlefeeding avoid storing or serving the milk in flexible plastic bottles, use glass instead. This is because some bendy plastics contain the ingredient phthalate, which if leached is implicated in altering hormones, so that male fish become feminised. Glass bottles are reasonably robust and have been successfully used for years. For instance in the classic *Baby and Childcare* first published in 1955, Dr Spock clearly talks about glass bottles and suitable ways to sterilise them (put in a saucepan and boil for two minutes). If you don't want the risk of breaking glass you can feed bigger babies expressed milk from a cup, or even teaspoon.

Also, there is a lack of clarity about the effects of microwave-heated food on growing cells and dentists warn that serving milk in a bottle after a baby is a year old can cause tooth decay. Switch Junior's bedtime soporific brew to a cold drink served in a cup before teeth get brushed.

Expressing keeps your milk supply up but it is another skill to learn, so practice before the end of your maternity leave. You may also find it more efficient to use an electric pump (which can be hired from your nearest NCT group) than to manually or hand express when you get to your office, where baby life often seems very removed. If finances and work allows, another option is to delay your return back to work so that your ability to breastfeed is not compromised before your baby's first birthday.

Do I need a steriliser?

I just steamed bottles in a big pan (pressure cooker). It's safer if you set the timer. I tried to do this task when I felt with it. No tablets involved and I didn't need an expensive steamer.

Anna, 36, with Freddie, four, and Elsie, two

Until recently the advice used to be sterilise anything used by a baby, from bottle teats to nappies. Surely no one sterilises nappies now, though parents are divided about whether to super-clean dummies and all the toys their babies chew every time something falls on to the floor. However, there's an obvious stage in your child's early life when you don't need to sterilise anymore… as soon as she starts crawling around the floor – especially if this is over a year – and is putting all sorts of bits and dirty fingers into her mouth. That's when basic hygiene ought to be good enough.

‘ I do sterilise, but looking forward to not having to! We use a cold water method and use the discarded water to flush down the sink to clear drains a bit, or to clean floors, or scrub decking. ’
Rita, 38, with Leo, two, and Rosa, two months

If you need to sterilise anything you don't need all that space-age equipment. Either add items to the dishwasher on a hot wash or put your breast pump, teats, bottles, etc., into a saucepan of cold water and bring to boil, then boil for two minutes. Or if you have a big saucepan that fits a metal vegetable steam tray you can get bottles to stand up regimentally and let them steam for around ten minutes.

Finding Seasonal and Local Food

It's easy to cut down the carbon footprint of your food if you use produce that hasn't been flown around the world, driven back and forwards from a depot to your nearest store and then kept in an open-shelved chiller section. A good start is to choose fruit and veg that is in season in the UK or Europe. Some shops promote locally grown produce but generally a supermarket shopping trip is season free.

You can find out what's in season by buying the right cookbook or even having a go growing your own. Or find a company that will deliver produce to your door once a week (find your nearest at http://vegbox-recipes.co.uk/veg-boxes/find-a-box-scheme.php). Veg box schemes are an easy way to get to know what grows when. A friendly greengrocer could help too – and help you find ways to survive the UK 'hunger gap', the time in April–May when local produce is hard to

Tips for eco-friendly eating habits

○ Eat food that's in season (ideally some should be organic) and point out ripe food to your child when you wheel the buggy past (bean wigwams in a front garden, plums on a tree). It should be even fresher if it is grown near to you.

○ Eat less meat and dairy (pork and chicken are usually low-carbon meats but it depends on how the animals have been raised and fed).

○ Raw food saves on cooking and retains more nutrients (try slices of apple, peach, satsuma, tomatoes, cucumber or grated courgette, carrot, etc., which can always be dipped into yoghurt/homemade tomato sauce/hummus).

○ Whole grains are low in fat – guide your child towards healthy eating patterns and they should enjoy a life with lower cholesterol/blood pressure and a reduced risk of cancer, diabetes and heart disease. Babies and young children do need some full fat food though.

○ Use up your leftovers (loads of ideas at www.lovefoodhatewaste.com) and compost all kitchen stuff/veg garden waste that you can't eat.

come by as it is still growing. As you find out more your baby will be learning too.

Having a weekly vegetable or fruit bag with contents you have no say about – other than they are seasonal – forces you to cook in a different way that doesn't suit everyone. But the pluses are that it saves time as there's no need to take the baby round the shops. It's also a great way to learn how to make tasty dishes from classic produce such as Jerusalem artichokes, kohl rabi, purple sprouting broccoli, celeriac and salsify.

Can you eat less meat and fish?

Intensive livestock farming for meat, dairy and eggs puts a ferocious strain on the environment because it requires so much water, pesticides and herbicides and is reliant on fossil fuels.

When weaning your baby nutritionists suggest you give at least one portion of red meat a week, and two of oily fish (see below), meaning that you don't have to feed your baby meat every day. You can include protein in a family veggie diet by offering pulses (lentils, kidney beans), soya and nuts (see warning on next page), as well as eggs and dairy. Ideally, you can also offer iron-rich foods at mealtimes with vitamin C (vegetables, fruit, potatoes or a splash of orange juice). Good sources of iron are baked beans, lentils (easy to include in soups and stews), spinach, wheatgerm and cabbage. Dried apricots and dates have loads of iron too and are a useful snack food.

Eating less meat is not just good for the planet: recent research shows that vegetarians have a reduced risk of cancer, diabetes and heart disease. Many families go a step further, and raise their children as vegans – indeed, one of most children's all-time-favourites, beans on toast, is a vegan meal.

'I'm a vegan and I made sure that I did my research while I was pregnant so that I could answer any questions about iron, protein, etc. My mind tends to go blank when people pose questions, so having a few answers ready really helped me. For me, trying to read top tips on websites and reading the books on raising vegan children, and also fact sheets on the Vegan Society www.vegansociety.com and Vegetarian Society, www.vegsoc.org, websites, really helped. I also tried to meet other vegans, either face-to-face or through the message boards on websites. I find it comforting to know others are experiencing the same issues and sharing ideas.'

Sharon, 40, with Saffron, nine

Although children love fish fingers and oily fish is billed as a superfood, deciding whether to keep serving it is a tough decision. I used to like serving salmon fishcakes and tuna bagels occasionally, but campaigner Charles Clover in his book and film, *End of the Line*, shows that fish stocks are perilously close to non-recovery. Even if two portions of oily fish a week give your baby all the omega-3s they need, it does not seem a fair trade off if your grandchildren won't get to eat fish. There are still some stocks of fish that are not at risk and good to eat, so if you love fish look at the Marine Stewardship Council's pocket shopping guide, which can be ordered at www.msc.org.

If you stop eating fish you can still serve up those essential fatty acids in cold-pressed vegetable oils (soya, corn and sunflower), avocados and margarine. They are also in olive, hemp and flax oil (also known as linseed). Nuts are good, but don't give any nuts to under ones, and be cautious when serving any child nuts in case of allergy. Animal-free omega-3 supplements are also sold in health food shops.

Family Meals

> With food, there are so many difficult decisions – air miles versus children's health and nutrition – but I want them to enjoy eating and trying out new tastes and interesting food, like mangoes. And then there's fair trade versus organic. The shop around the corner doesn't have MSC-label fish like Waitrose, but it's local and the fishmonger is so nice.
>
> **Sarra, 36, with Saskia, four, Alfie, two, and Ivan, three months**

> The reason we're running into obesity and diabetes epidemics is because we are eating too much, and because food is grown intensively which makes it deficient in vital nutrients. It's my opinion that those nutritional deficiencies have long-term consequences, including on our appetite.
>
> **Patrick Holden, 58, father of four grown-up children, and four young sons aged between two and nine, and Director of the Soil Association**

Watching a toddler tuck into their tea with gusto – perhaps puréed spinach with potato – is a pleasure. Six-month-olds and up have small stomachs and need to eat little and often to keep up their energy levels, but as toddlers become ever more active they need three meals as well as two or three snack times. At times this can seem like you've become your child's personal chef – not a good role if you feel they have insatiable appetites or a tendency to reject your offerings. Either save to use again, or compost. The basic diet changes you will need to cater for are:

○ 0–6 months: just breast milk (or formula).
○ 6–12 months: give breast milk plus a slow introduction of other foods. It's so exciting moving into the baby-feeding phase that lots of people rush, try to go slowly – a new taste for a couple of days – so it's easy to see if a particular food is creating an adverse reaction, other than a lip-curling, spitty removal.
○ 12 months onwards: family meals, healthy snacks as well as breast milk (or water to drink).
○ Two years onwards (or when ready): when you're at home teach your child to try new tastes and avoid waste. Get them naming vegetables and selecting fruit at the grocer's, supermarket or pick your own. They'll probably enjoy making muffins, kneading bread and licking spoons if you make it a game and ignore the mess. If you are growing food and they need a summertime snack try picking things fresh from your garden together, such as beans, tayberries and tomatoes.

Nutritious wholefoods are not what advertisers exhort us to eat. As a result there's a myth that shop-bought is best – even though it is likely to be preserved with salt and sugar, contain lots of fat and be over-packaged and pricey. There's no need to buy baby rice or jars of baby food because you'll end up having to throw out, compost or recycle so much of your purchase. Instead, offer smaller portions from your own meals.

Baby-led weaning – you offer breast milk and then finger foods rather than purées – is an uncomplicated way of getting your child eating the same things as the rest of the family. It's ideal if you have several children already, as you let the baby discover textures and tastes while feeding the rest. With their newly developed pincer grip, babies can hold on to hunks of bread, vegetable sticks or cubes, rice cakes and fruit. Meat and fish can also be served as finger foods.

' Babies get all the nutrients they need in breast milk, that's why they say "up to one food's just for fun". Baby-led weaning was fantastic because I could give Alfie things Saskia was already having, so he mushed and squished steamed carrot sticks, wedges of banana, toast and cooked pear. When he went to nursery at ten months they were amazed he could feed himself. Oranges, bananas, bread and raisins are good for when we are out and about. Jars and sachets of baby food were useful for snacks and I also used to freeze food in batches so I'd have food ready quickly if needed. '
Sarra, 36, with Saskia, four, Alfie, two, and Ivan, three months

Making purée (in a bigger bowl this would be an adult's hearty soup) is simplicity itself. Slightly overcook the veg, then decant most of the cooking water (you can also use this as a base for soups, stews, bread mix or as a very simple stock) and mush up the rest with a fork or hand-held blender. Salt should not be added to food for under-ones. I never add salt to my cooking, even if the recipe insists. If anyone finds this bland, they can always add salt to their own portion.

'You don't have to buy all your baby's food. Why buy oatcakes with all that salt, sugar and packaging when you can just mix oatmeal, fat and water? Your toddler can help you do it. I offer sliced carrots instead of bars full of sugar – but you could make the bars yourself using fruit or fruit purées. Look at what shops are selling to get ideas. Faith's taught me things too. She had all these tiny little containers of raisins and fruit and oatcakes and I thought my parents used to do this, too. Now I've learnt to take my sandwiches in Tupperware boxes when we go out in the car. It means we don't have to spend a fortune at service stations.'

Pip, 46, with Faith, three

Preparing a snack at home to enjoy when in the park when our baby gets hungry later helps us remember how much fun (and cheaper) family picnics can be. It's a formative experience that babies often have to remind us to do again.

'We were reading one of the old Topsy and Tim books, published in the 1950s, and the family stopped off during a long drive to have lunch. There were no service stations then so the mum handed the twins a paper bag with a hard-boiled egg, an apple and slices of bread in it. They had real linen napkins and squash or tea from a flask. It made me remember that's what my mum used to do – there were no plastic bottles of water to drink and then throw away, or sandwich wrappers to bin. There was no waste at all after a picnic.'

Julie, 45, with Freya, ten, and Clara, six

Water from a cup (or teaspoon) should be offered with every meal, and be available to your child whenever you think they are thirsty. The water companies have a legal obligation to provide safe tap water, although some people like to filter it as well. Buying bottles of water is wasteful and expensive so it is worth splashing out on a non-plastic water bottle you can carry around under the buggy or in your bag.

Raw goodness

Boiling and steaming food destroys some of the nutrients, which means that some of the healthiest (and most energy-efficient) snacks you can offer could be raw. (The exception is vitamin A, which is better absorbed when cooked – find it in carrots, spinach, green and yellow vegetables, fruit and dried apricots).

For a raw platter, try mashing ripe fruit such as banana, kiwi or mango. Courgette, carrot and apple all grate well and are nice to pick at. Avocado is rich in vitamin Bs and E. When they are in season soft fruit such as strawberries, raspberries and blackberries are often enjoyed by toddlers. Dried fruit will soften if left for an hour and up to overnight in water. You can buy overpriced packets of fruit salad and pre-sliced fruit at supermarkets so steal the idea and pre-slice mangoes, pears and tomatoes and then pop them in a plastic container to offer at snack time, perhaps with a bit of baguette. Or cut the load in your bag by buying fruit the baby and you like the look of at the moment you are ready to eat. (You can always carry a small bottle of water to clean greengrocer treats if you prefer to wash fruit and veg before eating.)

If you drink water and always offer it as a drink your child is unlikely to complain – and they can usually be tempted to drink something if you offer a straw. Resist pleas for squash (additive filled) and fizzy drinks (often riddled with sugar) so your children don't get in the habit of whining for special drinks whenever you are out. As your children grow older and are better able to reason you can adapt that rule. If you are really fussy about food, or watching the pennies, you can also freeze fruit juice or smoothies to make your own tasty lollies, which can avert the 'I want an ice cream' fight if your toddler knows they will get an icy treat when you get home as part of their tea.

Organic choices

Parents are almost hardwired to go to huge lengths to ensure their babies and very young children do not have their health or vitality compromised. It's a primal thing, really deep. I've got a grown-up family and four young boys under nine. My youngest, James, is nearly two so I've had a second reminder of the power of this desire. It's about positive health – not just about the nasties and what they don't want their babies to have in their diet – it's about what could promote positive vital health. All parents want to avoid food for their babies which might have pesticide residues or additives, but they also believe intuitively that food that is grown in a healthy soil is likely to be more nourishing. And I think that intuition is well grounded. Evidence is emerging that food grown without pesticides and with sustainable production methods, based on rotation, does actually have higher levels of trace minerals, antioxidants and essential fatty acids. **'**

Patrick Holden, 58, father of four grown-up children, and four young sons aged between two and nine, and Director of the Soil Association

Organic is today's food lodestar. It is grown without artificial fertilisers or pesticides and with consideration to the long-term health of the land and its wildlife. Research has found that organic farms boast more birds, beneficial insects and other wildlife. It offers surprising extra benefits to the consumer as well, for instance, research by the Universities of Liverpool and Glasgow (2002–2005) show that organic food contains higher levels of vitamin C and essential minerals such as calcium, magnesium, iron and chromium, as well as cancer-fighting antioxidants and omega-3. It's also been found that organic milk is on average 68% higher in omega-3 essential fatty acids. If you can only afford one organic item, opting for organic milk could give your whole family long-term benefits.

Certified organic food is often more expensive because it costs more to produce – although it depends where and how you buy it. Sharing a sack of organic potatoes with another family or two is a definite budget buy, although you will need enough space to store your haul. If you can only budget for a limited amount of organic produce, then buy the raw ingredients – whether these are milk, meat or vegetables/fruit – rather than a packaged meal.

Is organic better?

The Soil Association, the charity campaigning for planet-friendly food and farming, insists that organic food is nutritionally superior, so choosing organic means you get 'more carrot for your carrot'. The following comes from the Soil Association's Sam Allen. For more info see www.soilassociation.org.

Milk: 'Organic dairy production has huge benefits for health and the environment as well as animal welfare. New research of particular relevance to pregnant women and new mums regards the health benefits of organic milk, a pint of which contains on average 68.2% more total omega-3 fatty acids than conventional milk. Scientists in Holland discovered that infants fed on organic dairy products, and whose mothers also consume organic dairy, have a 36% lower incidence of eczema than children who consume non-organic dairy products. The charity Compassion in World Farming believes that the Soil Association's welfare standards are leaders in the field. The Soil Association bans the live export of calves, and requires high welfare standards for farmers who rear them. Because organic dairy systems do not push the cows to produce as much milk as non-organic herds, cows do not have to be culled as often, which eliminates the added emissions associated with frequent replacements for the herd.'

Veg box: 'Studies of organic food have shown that on average it has higher levels of iron, calcium, magnesium, phosphorus, chromium, vitamin C and a higher dry matter content – meaning you get more carrot for your carrot! If you want to save money try making meals from scratch using ingredients from your organic veg box. By buying direct from the farmer you can save money and get fresh, seasonal, organic food delivered straight to your door.'

Did you know there are no clear nutritional standards covering children's nurseries?

Organix and the Soil Association are calling on the Department for Children, Schools and Families (DCSF) to take responsibility for food in nurseries and develop mandatory national standards. You can join the campaign for Better Nursery Food at www.nurseryfood.org.

Childhood favourites

Leftovers can be transformed into childhood favourites if you go easy on instant composting – which you might if you feel your shopping bill is high. For example, spare portions of mash and cabbage cooked up again until it is creamy, crispy and steaming hot is such a delicious ending for leftovers that it is known by many names including the onomatopoeic bubble and squeak in England, colcannon in Ireland and rumbledethumps in Scotland. Like many favourite UK meals, including shepherd's pie, bread and butter pudding and cheese on toast, it is one that is best made from leftovers, rather than cooked from scratch. Below are some tasty ideas to help cut the amount of usable food thrown out:

○ Save potato and any water used to steam veg to cook lentils for stock, bread making, rice, risotto or to stretch a soup. Or use cool as a tea to nourish house plants or veg seedlings

- Almost-stale bread can be revived by running water over it and then putting in a hot oven for ten minutes. Or use up crusts/baguette ends by grating and then freezing the crumbs to use as toppings for cauliflower cheese, shepherdess pie, grilled tomatoes/mushrooms and reheated leftovers such as risotto, pasta or potato bake.
- Cheese, yoghurt, fromage frais and many other products can be frozen if you have too much to eat or are going away. Experiment.
- Root vegetables last well, but if they look less tasty try making a big dish of veg soup or stew, then freeze what you don't want to eat now.
- Grated celeriac, beetroot, cabbage and carrot make delicious cold, uncooked salads if you add olive oil. Beetroot leaves are a good addition to salads.
- Cereals keep better in airtight containers. Or switch to porridge oats to make breakfast a simple one-pot choice. Turn it into a treat by adding banana or raisins as you cook and then serve with a piece of melting chocolate or a swirl of yoghurt.

Find other tips at www.lovefoodhatewaste.com or swap your own ideas with friends.

Gardening

While I'm gardening Leo likes to decorate sticks/stakes; dig soil with plastic spoons; make "cakes" with old kitchen utensils and mud and stones; and make labels for plants.

Rita, 38, with Leo, two, and Rosa, two months

The simplest way to know where your food comes from is to grow your own – or at least some of your favourite fruit and veg. Growing your own is a real twenty-first-century trend, during 2009 even the Queen, Michelle Obama and Gordon Brown introduced veg plots at Buckingham Palace, the White House and Number 10. All have gardeners to do the hard work, but if you are on your own with a little baby you need to time gardening for when they sleep. As they get older they will help you a little, providing you offer lots of distraction – maybe a patch where they can create a mud world for model animals, trucks, dinosaurs, etc.?

> It's not too hard to garden with little children, especially as they're going to be in the pram/pushchair for the first part of it. Then I think if you're being realistic, it's distracting them rather than involving them in what you're doing. As toddlers, my girls always loved making mud pies, which meant a bucket, a bit of water and anything disgusting to put in it. A baby watering can is always a winner.
>
> Dominic Murphy, 44, author of *The Playground Potting Shed: a Foolproof Guide to Gardening with Children*

To be self-sufficient requires expert skill, whereas growing a few of your favourites is much more achievable. You need a bit of space, though a pot of mint, oregano and basil on a sunny windowsill is an exciting start. As your baby gets bigger, experimenting with different seeds and varieties (chard is easy and a great place to find shield bugs and other mini beasts) is almost as fun as watering your plot. Being able to grow just a little is empowering too. Green goddess Penney Poyzer, who starred in a BBC 2 show called *No Waste Like Home,* tries to eat something grown in her not very big Nottingham garden every day of the year. She has gluts when the salads are in season, but during the winter and spring months it'll be herbs such as sage and rosemary, a verbena (lemon mint) tisane or beans sprouted on a sunny windowsill.

' Gardening is quite easy if you are organised enough to put things in at the right time. Then I just water and hope it works. This year we're growing potatoes, tomatoes and courgettes in hanging baskets. We've got cut-and-come salads, herbs and on our roof loads of strawberries, blueberries and spring onions. There's a crab apple tree and a small pear tree (all in just ten-metre squared city garden). I told my husband that I can't do the gardening with the new baby so he's done it with the children and they love it '

Sarra, 36, with Saskia, four, Alfie, two, and Ivan, three months

Looking around allotments, it is clear that the best gardeners seem to be on the older side, so you could give your toddler a head start by starting them gardening young. If the slugs and snails eat your first efforts you can cheat by buying ready to crop plants – find them at a garden centre, DIY store, farmers' market, village fete or even from a neighbour.

If it's winter, or you haven't got a garden, try sowing cress on kitchen towel. Keep it in the light, and keep it damp. Or try sewing the seeds in the shape of your child's first initial. You can do this four or five days before a planned birthday party to give out as an alternative party bag.

Composting

You may already be composting kitchen scraps at home but increasingly many councils also offer food waste recycling. This is an excellent way of reusing chicken bones (once you've boiled them up for stock), unwanted meat (if you don't have a dog) and cooked plate scraps (if you haven't yet been tempted by backyard hens) as it is sent to municipal composters which reach much higher temperatures than home kits. Once rotted down into compost it may then be used in garden nurseries and parks in your area.

Well-rotted raw leftovers enrich your soil, making it more fertile, so if you are going to grow any plants it saves money to produce your own compost. Many councils offer subsidised compost bins so look at their websites to find out if your one does. For a quicker compost fix consider using a wormery. Wormeries create excellent compost tea and can provide your child with their first pet too.

‘ Leo likes putting banana skins, etc., in the wormery and he likes holding the worms. He's quite gentle with insects too. ’

Rita, 38, Leo, two, and Rosa, two months

Baby steps

Small

O Make a big pot of dinner and plan for leftovers. Purée and decant some into an ice-cube tray so you can freeze baby-sized portions and adult-sized portions of food (e.g., large yoghurt pot or lidded plastic containers) ready for when you are too tired to cook or baby too fretful to let you… Reuse the ice-cube tray by ejecting the frozen cubes into a clean food bag (even easier to get out of the freezer and into the pot).

○ Take a thermos with you so that you can have a hot drink in the park or keep kettle water hot back home.

○ Thrifty cooks use lids and only turn the oven on when food is inside. Also fill the oven with different dishes so you use your heat in the most efficient way. As you cook jacket potatoes you can also squeeze in roasting veg, crutons, a cake, flapjacks and heat up baked beans and frozen peas. Pasta cooks once brought to boil, just turn off the heat and time for normal cooking length to save electricity.

Medium

○ Eat more vegetarian meals (see recipes at www.vegsoc.org) or try out some vegan recipes (see recipes at www.vegansociety.com).

○ Waste less: try out as many ideas as you can to avoid throwing away edibles. As a last resort, compost.

○ Sow a few plants with your child. Radishes are easy, as are cut and come again salads if well watered. Rocket and mizuna are quite spicy greens but easy to grow. Or try nasturtiums, which look pretty and can be added to salads.

Large

○ Buy a worm bin or order tiger worms from a compost supplier. You now have easy to maintain pets, and by adding the right sort of kitchen scraps the worms thrive creating a rich juice (worm wee?) which you collect from a tap at the bottom of the container and use as a fertiliser to boost plant growth.

○ Set yourself challenges. Can you eat something you've grown or made every day? Can you garden organically? Can you preserve food when there's a glut or it is cheap in shops (e.g., make jams, marmalade, pickles or use a freezer to lengthen shelf life of your bought and homemade meals)?

Five
Nappies

Although the main option in the shops seems to be disposable nappies, there is a head-spinning range of alternatives that are also often cheaper. There is no doubt that disposable nappies are more convenient – but if you choose washables there are ways to conquer those seemingly endless mountains of nappies. Read on for the bottom line on nappy, and no-nappy, know-how.

For anyone watching their cash and concerned about the environment, washable nappies are the obvious choice. A study by the Environment Agency and WRAP in 2008 estimated that a baby wearing nappies will need eight changes a day at birth, reducing to about four by two and a half years; that's around 4,500 nappy changes. Choose disposables and you will need to pay for 4,500 nappies. Opt for washables and you might only need 30. However, doing that laundry yourself is going to be a bit more work than just popping down to the supermarket when you run out of nappies.

Your nappy choice will depend on how much help you have, how healthy you and your baby are, who helps you, how much your baby wees and how many nappy (and clothing) changes you are willing to make each day. All nappies leak sometimes, fasteners wriggle free and unspeakable – but very pongy – bodily functions leave their mark in exactly the places you wouldn't want.

For lots of reasons parents often put their new arrival in a disposable nappy. If you are giving birth in a hospital without access to your washing machine or line dryer this makes absolute sense. But once back at home it can seem tricky to switch from disposables to a greener nappy. Yet if we all tried to choose the method least harmful to the planet there wouldn't be eight million nappies each year taken to landfill sites, where they take hundreds of years to rot down.

My family's nappy system CASE STUDY

Until you've had to change nappies frequently, it is hard to figure out the right routine. Here's what I did: Pete and I lived in a tiny flat with no outside space when my first daughter was born, and we were still there nearly three years later when number two arrived. We changed Lola's nappy on the floor in the sitting room (she used washables by day and a compostable disposable at bedtime). We stored dirty washable nappies in a bucket in the bath. The lid stayed on but it didn't smell too bad, thanks to the two drops of lavender or tea tree oil that I'd add before putting in the first dirty nappy (about six filled the bucket). At first I soaked the nappies in water, but it was a real faff tipping the dirty water out before they went into the washing machine in the kitchen. After about a year I realised that not soaking the nappies was far easier, and the nappies still came up clean. This system is called dry pailing and used for just wet or dirty nappies and also for nappies to be collected by a laundry service.

The Nappy Options

Like so much of parenting, the nappy system you pick on day one may not be what you are using by day three or even the third month. It's not a sign of weakness to rethink what nappy system best suits your family.

What's filling my pants?

Type	Disposable nappies	Reusable cloth nappies
What's in the nappy?	Mix of wood pulp, cloth, plastic, chemical gels and adhesives for most disposables. The biodegradable brands may include maize (GM risk), bamboo and wood pulp (if FSC-certified, should come from well-managed sources).	Variety of new and pre-used materials can be found – including cotton, bamboo and hemp. Materials tend to be compostable but may not be grown in a sustainable way (e.g., cotton crops need large amounts of water).
Is it reusable?	No.	Yes, many times and on more than one child.
Can I make each nappy last longer?	Sometimes. Use parcel tape to reseal (e.g., if you thought the baby had done a poo and it turns out to be a false alarm).	Shake poos out, add a new (washable) liner and then put back on.

Does it add to greenhouse gases?	Yes, during manufacture, shipping and disposal.	Washables use 40% less carbon dioxide in making and disposal than conventional, non-biodegradable disposables.
What will I have to do?	Buy nappies each week and carry them home. Cost: pounds.	Choose and buy cloth nappies. Dispose of poos, wash and dry nappies or sign up to a laundry service. Not expensive.
Best method of disposing?	Secure in biodegradable bag and put in household rubbish bin.	If nappy is in good condition store, sell or pass on. If worn out recycle in textile bin.

1. Disposable nappies

Green score – low

Many parents like disposables because they are convenient, very absorbent and make baby care simple. The problem is that every year there are 1.7 million babies in nappies – and nine out of ten of them are using disposables. In a landfill dirty disposables take hundreds of years to rot down. They degrade even slower if people have sealed them in a plastic bag and then put them inside another household rubbish bag ready for the bin men.

On the plus side disposables are so absorbent that by the time your child has had their first birthday and is able to walk, you may find that you only need to throw away one nappy each day, especially if you are able to organise some regular chunks of nappy-free play. From a year on if your child passes solid faeces, you may also be able to shake the poo down the loo and then flush, efficiently bypassing the landfill route.

Lots of families use a mix of disposable and reusable nappies. You might find a disposable more convenient at night or if you or your child is ill, when you travel or are visiting friends or relations. However, you can be more environmentally savvy by using a partially biodegradable disposable, also available at most supermarkets.

2. Disposable nappies – partially biodegradable
Green score – medium

Part-biodegradable disposable nappies are a real boon for parents looking for something a bit greener than a conventional disposal, but don't feel ready to try washables at every nappy change.

The 70% compostable Nature Babycare nappy brand was created nearly 30 years ago when Marlene Sandberg was on maternity leave from her job in Sweden. Marlene was so shocked by the difficulty of finding compostable nappies for her babies that she decided to set up a company determined to 'make a high-performance nappy that was more friendly to nature and healthier for the child'. The result was Naty, a company specialising in greener baby care products. The nappies, Nature Babycare, are sold in supermarkets throughout the world. They look similar to disposable brands, but boast a back sheet that is made of GM-free maize, bio film and FSC-certified tree pulp. The company also produces fully compostable nappy bags.

The drawbacks are that compostable nappies are not quite as good at rotting down as you might imagine (they will take many months in your home composter or wormery). They can also be more expensive so bulk buy, so share costs with a friend when you see special offers.

To dispose of a dirty, partly compostable nappy seal up the tapes then put into your normal rubbish bin, ideally lined with a biodegradable plastic bin liner. You can also check what your council would like you to do with part-biodegradable nappies as it may be happy to let you place soiled nappies into your green waste bins.

3. Washable nappies

Green score – high

' Real nappies are made of natural fabrics so don't contain the gels, glues, bleach, plastics and perfumes that go into disposables. If I didn't want Leo's food to contain chemicals, it seemed natural that his nappies shouldn't, either. But the thing that clinched it for me was the cost – you can kit out your baby in real nappies for under £50 and these can last for your baby's "nappy lifetime". To buy enough disposables costs about £900! I found out my council offered a subsidy of £54, so if I didn't like the washables, then at least I wouldn't be out of pocket. I've bought a few additional nappies since then, but I've still saved a huge amount and now I'm using them on number 2. '
Rita, 38, with Leo, two, and Rosa, two months

Modern washables are not at all fiddly to put on. It takes seconds to layer a cloth nappy with the booster pads and poo-catching flushable or washable liner, and then you secure with poppers or Velcro. They last and last too. One washable nappy can be reused on at least two babies, maybe more, which makes washables a budget buy. And when they're eventually worn out they can be recycled in textile bins. Fans of washables flag up their softness, absorbency, comfort, planet-friendly and chemical-free credentials.

There are a huge range of cloth nappy options from all-in-ones (which can take longer to dry) to foldable squares where you essentially build the nappy by adding liners until you have the absorbency level your baby needs. The drawback is that they require more work because your laundry pile increases.

You will also need the space to store dirty nappies (ideally, without water in a lidded bucket) until you are ready to do a wash. You will also have to peg the nappies up to dry. It's not hard to do, although it may take some trial and error to get your drying system working. Or you can sign up to a nappy laundering service.

I'll be honest: it's a bit harder at first using washables than disposables. But persevere and it will soon become second nature. In fact, cloth-wearing babies often nappy train earlier, which is a bonus. If you need practical advice about dealing with washables, from leaks to washing crises, call the Real Nappy Helpline on 0845 850 0606, www.realnappy.com. Another good website to check out is The Nappy Lady, www.thenappylady.co.uk, which offers home visits so you can match your baby's gender and drying arrangements with the best washable nappy.

4. Washable nappies from a nappy laundry service

Green score – very high

If you would like to choose the washable nappy option, but are concerned about coping with extra laundry or lack of drying space, then using a nappy laundry service is a perfect choice, and even greener than doing the washing at home. A nappy laundering service will supply and deliver the correct size of prefolded nappies to your home, and collect dirty nappies on a pre-arranged date each week – so you don't need to do any washing or drying.

A nappy laundry service costs about the same each week as buying disposable nappies. However, some councils offer a grant, making this real value for money. If you have a service nearby then this is the way to go – not only does it save wear and tear on your own washing machine, it saves you money if you're on a water meter – as well as being the best eco option, thanks to economies of scale.

5. Elimination communication – the no-nappy system

Green score – very, very high

Ana and I hadn't read hundreds of baby books before our baby was born, but we did read *Diaper Free*. We weren't sure when to start, but at two weeks Harri got slight nappy rash, so the health visitor said keep his nappy off. We held him over a large container (we often use the toilet now) and made a cueing noisee – a hiss for a wee and a grunt for a poo. Ana's grandmother, who is Welsh, said "we used to do that". It's only recently that nappies came in. Most of the world did or does what we do with Harri – from the Welsh valleys to Africa. *'*

Gamal, 35, and Ana, 24, with Harri, seven months

Elimination communication (EC) is a toilet-training system where parents learn to recognise when their babies poo and wee through a mix of observation and intelligent guesswork. As a result they are able to get their baby to wee and poo over a container. This is a brilliant way of dealing with your baby's excrement as it cuts down on the amount of nappies that need washing and empowers your baby to communicate with you when he needs to go, rather than become nappy trained. Families who use this method say that their children are potty trained much earlier than those using nappies.

EC is a skill which you and your partner could learn together. It's not really a no-nappy system as you do use nappies (especially when you are out and about) in case of accidents, but you pay attention to your child so that you are able to let them use a potty at the right moment. You help too by giving a regular cue (a hiss or a grunt). Discovering how your child communicates her need for the toilet means that you establish communication early on – but many parents who use EC say that they really bond with their children over this practice.

The bible for elimination communication is *Diaper Free: The Gentle Wisdom of Natural Infant Hygiene* by Ingrid Bauer. If you're interested in this method, read *Diaper Free* a couple of months before your baby is born as it works most effectively if you give it an early start. Also see www.ehow.com, www.theecstore.com and videos on YouTube that show very young babies weeing when a hissing cue is made. If you've never come across elimination communication before it will give you a good laugh but it may just possibly take you on a very different child-rearing path that doesn't condemn your baby to two years in soggy nappies.

> I didn't think no nappies was an option despite having travelled a lot to places where the babies didn't seem to wear nappies. Then my mum sent me a newspaper article about EC. I googled it and found a whole new world to me: www.tribalbaby.org was really useful for finding out more information and *Diaper Free* is a great book. It is not about doing away with nappies, it is about tuning into your baby's needs and responding accordingly. We use nappies at certain times like for long journeys or when we're out and about or at someone else's house.
>
> Rachel, 39, with Jude, ten, and Eve, 14 months

Best and worst nappies

Best
Borrowed washables or a laundry service that provides nappies
New washables
Compostable disposables
Disposables
Washables dried with a tumble drier
Worst

So You've Decided on Washable Nappies

You've looked at the options and you've seen that the cheapest, most environmentally friendly option is the washable nappy. Perhaps you've decided on a mix of washable nappies backed up by compostable nappies.

> I'm using cloth nappies for the first time with child number three and of course now I'm using them I wonder why I didn't before.
>
> Laura, 42, with Alice, five, Tara, three, and Fergus, one

Switching from disposable to washable nappies can be done any time, and lots of families make the change once they feel confident dealing with their baby. Lara Adeagbo, an outreach worker for the Nappy Ever After laundry service, has heard all the worries mums have about trying a washable nappy. 'Some people think that a cloth nappy is not hygienic, or it might be itchy. Some think they still have to use pins and boil nappies. Some think their partners will be worried. But if a nappy is just wet (and it usually is because you catch the poo in a flushable

Tip

You can buy biodegradable nappy liners designed to flush down the toilet. However, they are strong enough to go in the washing machine once or twice, and you can also line disposables with them to make them last longer.

liner) then you just wash it with your normal laundry, or if you get your nappies collected by a laundry service you don't have to do anything except put it in a bucket. You don't even rinse the nappy.'

Washables typically come in three sizes, so you will need 15 newborn-sized cloth nappies, but less of the larger sizes as your child grows. So you will probably need 30 nappies between birth and potty training. Have a look on the internet

Tip

Make your own washables

If you need to be really budget conscious, you could try making your own washable nappies. Here's how Cristiano, 35, dad of Electra, 16 months, managed: 'I made ten nappies (from a mix of cotton and towelling) for £11 – the amount it would cost to buy one reusable nappy. My partner showed me a nappy she'd used on her first child (now five) and I just copied it. It took about 15 minutes.'

- ❍ To do this you need to find a style you like for a template (a basic all-in-one wrap with liners added for absorbency is going to be easier than a stuffable pocket design).
- ❍ Cut out something similar (newspaper can be useful to make a pattern), securely hem the edges and add Velcro fastenings. You can improve the fit with extra liners or by adding a folded muslin.
- ❍ In addition, there are countless sewing patterns for diapers and nappies on the web. See Resources for more information.

for the bumper packs that will take you from birth to potty training with a one-size-fits-all nappy (suitable for babies between 3.5–15 kg) or have a go with a starter pack which will have three to five nappies in the size you want. Or look out for second-hand nappies from friends and family. The real plus of acquiring second-hand washables is that you don't have to pre-wash and dry them three or four times to kick-start their absorbency. And since they've been used on a friend or neighbour's baby, you can call them if you have any questions.

Solving nappy crises

Any nappy leaks occasionally. Frequent leaks from a washable can be sorted by changing the style of fold in your chosen nappy, adding padding (e.g., insert booster pads folded thicker at the front for a boy; thicker at the back for a girl); switching nappy sizes; checking the nappy hasn't worked loose; repopping poppers or upgrading wrappers or plastic overpants. If a nappy is leaking because it's a bit big you can try stuffing it with extra booster pads, or improvise with a muslin, fleece or cut-up bath towel. Remember that brand-new cloth nappies will need to be washed a few times to fluff up and gain absorbency – just like you would do with a new towel.

> Try using terry towels when your baby is first born (perhaps for the first two or three months) so you can make the nappy fit snugly. Then after nappy nattering with friends and other families pick up some shaped washable nappies that you use time after nappy-changing time.
>
> Gisella, 37, with Lucas, seven, and Ivo, five

Another issue that you may not realise at first is that cloth nappies are bulkier than disposables so you'll have to make allowances when you buy baby clothes. If your friends and family plan on making or giving you baby clothes, let them know that you're using washables so they can to buy or make bigger sizes.

> Only thing I've found challenging about washable nappies is getting clothes to fit. I always have to double-check sizes. And Billy's birthday/Christmas presents are often designed with disposables in mind – there's not a chance he'd get his bum in. I like the brand Cut4Cloth (now Frugi, www.welovefrugi.com), as they are designed for use with cloth nappies. I've bought a few of these off eBay.
> Jo, 34, with 17-month Billy

Washing your nappies

> When my husband ran Fresh & Wild there was a newspaper article about how I put my washable nappies in with his shirts. People were shocked, but it didn't matter at all with the damp nappies (the dirty ones went in separately). I just soaked them with a bit of tea tree oil and then threw them into the washing machine.
> Tara, 37, with Olivia, ten, Eve, seven, and Orla, four

Washing nappies at home can have a big impact on your water usage and electricity bills if it is done thoughtlessly. The least efficient washing machines may use 70 litres per wash, while machines with an energy efficiency rating of A+ are more likely to use around 46 litres each full wash. To keep your family's carbon footprint and power bill down, aim to:

- Wash cloth nappies when there's a full load
- Upgrade to an A+ washing machine
- Wash at 40°C (not hotter)
- Line dry
- Avoid using the tumble dryer (don't even get one)
- Reuse outgrown nappies on another child

A dirty nappy can be horrible, but washables smell less than you might fear because you flush the poo away with the biodegradable liner (or just shake the poo off and wash the liner to reuse). Store dirty nappies (they are usually just wet) in a bucket with a lid. There's no need to soak the nappies if you are going to wash them within a few days.

Nappies soiled with poo from a milk-fed baby start yellow and then go magically white when dried in sunlight. However, if you are using lower temperatures and an eco-washing powder/liquid brand you will not end up with dazzling white clothes. Avoid choosing white nappies or little baby garments if you can't endure them turning slightly grey.

Drying

Washables take about 24 hours to dry in your house but if you tumble dry this negates the good eco impact of using washables. If you cannot air dry at home, then avoid nappies you have to wash or instead use a laundry service. If you keep your home quite cool, or rarely use radiators, it may be worth choosing the cloth nappies that dry fastest, such as cotton, terry towelling and fleece, or washables with separate booster pads. All-in-ones and the more absorbent hemp and bamboo take longer.

If you don't have a garden with a washing line or the weather is bad try using a yacht dryer. Essentially, they are a dozen clothes pegs attached to two/three small rings that can be hooked to dry small items anywhere. Use where hot air is rising, such as the stair well/banisters/curtain rail). Yacht dryers can also save time if you use an outside washing line but don't fancy unpegging every sock, bib and nappy at the first hint of rain.

Other ways to dry include using wooden slatted ceiling dryers (sometimes known as a Lazy Susan or Sheila Maid), which can be winched up out of the way (good places to put these are over stairs or the bath). In winter you can use brackets that hook on to your radiators. Drying racks that fold up when not in use are great and very popular in European apartments.

Tip

If you tumble dry your washables, iron them or repeatedly use a not-very-full older washing machine on a 60°C (or hotter) setting, your washable nappy choice stops being green.

How to change a nappy

As you'll be doing around eight nappy changes a day, organise a nappy-changing area near a tap, loo and your store of clean, folded nappies. If your bathroom is too small, find another spot, ideally on the floor, as that way your baby cannot roll over and accidentally fall. Beside the nappy-changing mat keep a bottle of tap water, or a plastic bowl and a damp flannel to wipe up spills, a muslin/hand towel to dab your baby's bum dry and a place to put down a soiled nappy.

You can place your baby on a folded towel, but a wipeable changing nappy mat makes life easy if poo gets accidentally smeared in places you'd rather it didn't (and it will). Poo can be removed with a muslin, toilet paper or a sponge (rinse or machine wash to clean), and it can be soaked out by leaving the offending item overnight in a small amount of water which you then tip down the loo. You don't need to super hot wash.

Nappy wipes

Save money by refusing to purchase wipes, or only using them when your baby has done a poo. When you buy wipes store them in a lidded container so that they don't dry out. You can dab your baby's bum with a wet flannel and then dry with a muslin/towel. Have lots of flannels or cut-up towels so you can use a clean one whenever you want to.

Some families use a washable flannel but dose it with a nappy-wipe spritz mix to make cleaning off the poo/wee easier.

There are lots of recipes for nappy wipes on the web. Most suggest starting with a lidded container and a roll of kitchen tissue. Cut this in half (easier said than done), remove the tube and then marinate the kitchen towels in your chosen mix, which might include cooled boiled water, camomile tea, olive oil or tea tree oil.

> A nappy mat is something I really couldn't do without. Your baby will spend a fair amount of time, especially in the early weeks, on their back having a nappy change, so they may as well be comfortable. And a plastic covered one will protect your floor, bed – wherever you do the change.

Rachel, 39, with Leila, four, and Ravi, 17 months

Once you get the hang of it, changing a baby's nappy can be a lovely time to chat, sing and cuddle your baby.

Tip

Some dads can feel overwhelmed when faced with changing nappies. As much as they'd like to help they can feel edged out by their partner, who has often spent more time with the baby and therefore has more experience. Remember that changing a nappy is a skill that needs to be learnt, and it's okay if it's not perfect on the first go.

If this is an issue in your home try to empathise and suggest a couple of days of nappy workshop where the one who doesn't want to do nappy changing does more than their fair share, perhaps for a suitable reward – you can have fun thinking it up.

Nappy networking

Many new mums find themselves with loads of questions – and that's where events known as nappuccinos or nappy natters can help. Nappuccinos are a great place to ask all those nappy-related questions, such as how do I wash them? Do I have to soak my nappies? What about nappy rash? They can also show you how to make boy or girl folds to stop the nappy leaking, tell you what nappy or laundry-service grants are available from your council and your nearest local supplier. And you'll meet other new mums.

> I want to be environmental but the nearest shop stocks Pampers. It's a slog up to the supermarket that sells a biodegradable brand and then the size I want always seems to be out of stock so I'm thinking of switching to washable nappies. That's why I came to the nappuccino, to find out more.
>
> Lizzie, with three-month-old son

Nappies out and about

If you like being outside, and are often a long way from baby-changing facilities, put together a portable changing kit so that you can sort out your baby's nappy anywhere. Having a portable nappy changing kit can save you from having to interrupt fun in the outdoors to find somewhere with baby-changing facilities. It may also mean that you avoid dealing with the dilemma of whether you can use these facilities and bolt or need to buy a cuppa and cake as an expensive thank you.

In the kit include:

○ Spare clean nappies (and one extra, just in case)
○ Spare set of dry clothes (especially bottoms)
○ Waterproof changing mat
○ Bag to store wet or dirty nappies

○ Small bottle of tap water and some cotton wool balls (or a washable flannel kept in a bag or Tupperware container, or nappy wipes)

○ Nappy-changing bag that stores everything above. Ideally, choose a bag that hooks over your buggy handles or is compact enough to fit underneath it. If you are mostly using a sling you can put your nappy bag into a rucksack. As grass and park benches are often damp and public conveniences often don't seem clean enough to place your newborn, it makes good sense to choose a waterproof, wipe-clean, fold up changing mat that doubles as a clean nappy holdall. You can make your own by adapting an old favourite bag, or buy new for about a tenner

Things you won't need

No matter what nappy system you mostly use, there are items that you do not need to waste money on:

○ **Nappy wrappers and powered nappy-disposal systems** – posh bins that tightly wrap up a disposable nappy supposedly to remove odours and seal up germs. These are not that easy to use and it is expensive to refill the **nappy cartridge**. Use an ordinary rubbish bin rather than wrapping a sealed plastic bag around your dirty nappy, which compounds the problem that disposable nappies take hundreds of years to decompose (the same goes for throwing dirty nappies out in a tightly knotted plastic bag).

○ **Nappy bags** – a string bag that you put into a nappy bucket and then fill with soiled washable nappies because it makes it easier to put your dirty washable nappy crop into the washing machine. How?

○ **Bleach** should not be used on washable nappies. Try line drying stained nappies in sunlight (even daylight can be enough) and you will be amazed how breastfed yellow infant poo vanishes. It's almost as good as a magic trick.

○ **Fabric conditioner** reduces the absorbing qualities of washable nappies. If they get stiff try line drying outside, or when they are drying inside give them a bit of a squeeze to regain that softer feel.

Potty Training

'You've got to make potty training fun – my mother told me I got the knack when I found I could pee through the railings on the veranda in Trinidad. You need lots of pairs of trousers – ones that they have just grown out of – and loads of terry towels on hand. Consider meditation and/or medication for parents who fail to see why their apparently delightful and intelligent child is unable to recognise the need to pee or poo until about five seconds after it has started.'

Hugh, 42, with Mati, six, and Pip, three

Early potty training means using less nappies. However, potty training is easier to do when there's no pressure, during warmer weather and at a point when your child is ready (between two and a half and three and a bit years). If you've been using washable nappies you're already at an advantage as disposables wick the moisture away, making it hard for your toddler to tell when he's wet himself.

Although there are reusable pull-ups that could save you the trouble of all those wet clothes, it is said to be easier for a child to become potty trained if they are wearing pants rather than thick nappy material. The problem is that it's quite hard for children to learn to be by the potty when they need to go – beautifully captured in Tony Ross's book about a little princess, *I Want My Potty!*

When you are potty training expect an increased wash load. Your child will make lots of mistakes, so collect up a pile of pants and trousers/leggings. Your task will be much easier if you haven't recently handed on the skirts, tights and trousers that they've almost grown out of.

Remember that it is likely to be another year before your potty-trained child is dry by night. It will save you a lot of drying time if you cover her mattress in a waterproof sheet and/or a waterproof mattress cover (and maybe have one spare for the very bad nights). Don't be too hasty taking these wraps off as illness, upset, moving house, fizzy drinks, water late in the day or being unable to do a wee at bedtime can all trigger another nighttime puddle.

The experts are united on this: to potty train successfully you need to be consistent, and don't get cross, it's no big deal. When you are out carry lots of pants and trousers. Use a towel if your child is going to be out of their nappy in a buggy or car seat that you mind being made wet. Let them watch you going to the loo, and when they do a wee or poo allow them to help you tip their potty contents into the pan and then flush (or help you tip cold bath water down the pan).

The potty

Potties are easy to borrow, and if you are going to have a child-friendly house it might be an idea to keep an old potty in a reasonably easy-to-locate place so that younger visitors aren't caught short. You can also buy a wide range of potties, including fold-up-flat portable models (just insert a biodegradable bag when your child or their friend wants to use it) that fit under your buggy until needed.

If your home is big or has two floors organise an upstairs potty and a downstairs one. Ideally, keep the potty close to where your child is busy. And when it's filled up empty it at once. If you are close to the compost heap you could add the wee to improve nitrogen levels.

'I bought a travel potty at an NCT sale. It has three layers. A seat with holes at the bottom for liquid to go through, a base and a seal-tight lid. It's been great for journeys, camping and I'll keep it in the pram for Pip's potty training.'

Zoe, 39, with Mati, six, and Pip, three

Potty training out and about

Make your outings easier by carrying a potty with you, or knowing where all the neighbourhood loos are located. Most children will wee or poo after eating so take them to the toilet after a meal or a big drink. Many people strongly dislike seeing small children making wee mistakes. So if you are in a park while potty training, aim to get your little one to use a potty (tipping the contents down a street drain or into a toilet pan when you can) unless there is no alternative.

The occasional al fresco wee is no problem, but poo should always be buried or, better still, carried back home. In national parks in the US it is standard practice to carry out your own excrement in a Tupperware. Just make sure that you know which one is for number twos and which gets used for storing sandwiches...

Baby steps

Small

◯ Try using a packet of compostable nappies rather than the ordinary disposables for a week or so.

◯ Get yourself a waterproof nappy changing mat so you can change nappies wherever you are – no excuses now to stop you going out.

◯ Take your baby to a nappy natter or nappuccino and ask all the questions you've got about washable nappies.

Medium

◯ Catch poo in a flushable liner and put into the loo (no need for nappy sacks). If you can manage this then you could probably switch to washable nappies (borrow one or two, or order a trial pack). Make sure you have sorted out your home drying system.

◯ Find out if there's a nappy laundry service near you. Ask for a brochure or price list.

◯ Ring your council (or ask a health visitor) and ask if you can get a grant for using washable nappies or for a nappy laundry service.

Large

○ Make and use your own wipes (or try clean ups with a flannel).

○ Try to let your little baby have some regular nappy-free playtime – it's a really good way of preventing and healing nappy rash.

○ Go diaper free (if not all the time, occasionally). Read up on elimination communication and try to interpret your baby's needs better so you can use less nappies. More info at www.diaperfreebaby.org/news.htm.

○ Become a real nappy champion: ambassadors are required by Naturewise, Real Nappy Information Service, councils, etc. – pick the sort you feel works best for you and be prepared to answer new mums' questions.

Six
Time with Your Baby

Maternity leave and the early months of baby care are a chance for you to discover play again, to find creative ways to multitask and learn to walk that bit slower and rediscover the world while your children are just beginning to explore it. It's a big learning curve – so this chapter reveals how families spend time with their children.

' For me, being a green parent isn't about killing myself over the details, but about instilling in my children a sense of wonder about the world and environment, a gentle sense of responsibility towards the environment and a sense of normality about living in a green way, not making it into an issue but just quietly getting on with it so that green awareness is part of their basic make-up. '
Hannah, 34, with Iola, three, and Cai, ten months

Going green means spending less and being informed about what you choose to buy. However, having a baby means that you are suddenly confronted with loads of plastic toys, DVDs and educational games – many designed to heighten parents' guilt if they don't have the latest 'must-have' accessory. By saying no to excess consumerism you are providing a huge first step towards your baby's ability to understand that it's OK to make things, experiment and cobble together – rather than buying it all new. Reassure yourself that you are not wrecking your baby's chance to be a genius – after all, did baby Einstein grow up bashing a computerised ABC or a funky foots play mat?

Breastfed newborns sleep a lot, alternating sleep and milk so tightly there's almost no time to admire them. But by the time they are six weeks old and rewarding you with their smiles, you can start to enjoy tried and tested favourite baby games such as rolling a big soft ball (or try scrunched-up newspaper), peek-a-boo, singing, rhymes and the absolute favourite, knocking over towers, as well as anything that involves exploration.

Toys and tidy-up time

As your baby grows let her play experimentally with things you already use, such as wooden spoons, wrapping paper, keys, board books, anything that can be safely touched, sniffed, mouthed and examined. So long as you are giving your baby love, food and attention she will be learning.

A lovely homemade item is a basket/box packed with natural objects that allow the baby to enjoy different textures. Make it yourself, or suggest Granny has a go.

> I made my grandson Billy a magic bag made out of blue velvet. Into it I put a toy gazelle, shaky African egg, oyster shell, whisk, sponge, bangle, loofah, brush, wood napkin ring, glittery stick and two 30-cm lengths of chain. Billy loves taking things out of it.
> Mary, 60, with four grandchildren

An adaptation of this – and a good way of keeping a room tidy – is to put your baby's toys in one or two big baskets or boxes that they can have fun unpacking as they play. Once they can move around encourage your child to help you tidy up too. Even if you do most of the work your older baby/toddler is likely to be pleased to have been asked and willing to give tidying up a go.

' The secret with toys has been to keep a small selection of favourites out all the time and rotate other toys every month or so. Finn never tires of re-discovering toys he's forgotten he had. And like any child, Finn likes his telly but with so many TV shows available online you can select your child's telly and avoid buying DVDs. '

Elaine, 44, with Finn, two, and Niall, two weeks

If you can't stand noisy toys ration or lose them. If you want to up the tempo you could dance around singing your own favourite songs, or turn on the radio.

Fun recipes for playing

Play dough

- ◯ Cup of flour
- ◯ Cup of water
- ◯ Add half a cup of salt if you want to stop your craft being eaten
- ◯ Big spoon (or 2 dessert spoons) of vegetable oil
- ◯ Optional: drop of food dye (or beetroot juice)

Mix together, then roll into snakes, balls, etc., or stick things into it. Store in an airtight container to prevent it from drying out. When it's ruined put in your compost bin.

Cornflour gloop

- ○ Cup of cornflour
- ○ Little bit of water
- ○ Optional drop of food dye

Stir together in a bowl then tip into a baking tray (or dish with sides). Then let your child touch and stir the mix, which changes texture in a fascinating way. You can add more water or cornflour to see what happens. When the mixture dries it goes powdery so is easy enough to clean up.

Snail racing

Hunt for at least one snail (snails aren't that easy to find in the winter). If you cannot tell your snails apart by size/pattern write a number on their shell with marker pen. Keep them in a damp, cool place with some food (lettuce or cabbage leaves) while you make a racetrack – and then begin the snail racing. Make sure you're gentle with them.

Consciously creative

I have two big boxes of every kind of pen, paint, coloured card, saved birthday and Christmas cards and anything that is glittery/feathery/has the potential to be used in a card or picture. Nothing gets wasted! Having children has given me a fantastic excuse to spend hours messing about with pens and paints, which I loved doing as a child. '

Elaine, 44, with Finn, two, and Niall, two weeks

Doing things with your children that you really used to enjoy, like drawing, sewing, singing or woodwork, but got out of the habit in early adulthood, is one of life's absolute pleasures. Arty stuff such as doodling and crafts are wonderful ways to pass time. Toddlers love doing shows, especially in costume, so provide them with a dressing-up box and you'll get the chance to be a theatre audience most days.

Make beauty or poison potions

A fun way to experiment with smells, textures and (when safe) tastes. You can store scented oils and creams in sterilised glass jars and maybe even present them as gifts.

Bath fizz

- 2 teaspoons sodium bicarbonate
- 1 teaspoon citric acid
- 2 drops essential oil (rose or lavender are always nice) a few dried petals
- Mix and keep in tin foil until you want to use in a bath.

Make a scrap store

Keep PV glue, Prit stick, paint, material scraps and cardboard boxes for art projects. Use them to create your own unique castle/café. Just as wood warms you twice – once when you chop it up and then when you burn it – so a creative endeavour can excite your child's imagination through collecting up usable scraps that can be transformed into something they can use for play. Creating your own castle (or café) aged two is an impressive introduction to green building.

Learn to sew

Punch holes in card in the shape of a simple outline like a fir tree, dog or person and then help your child learn to handle a needle and thread (or thread a shoelace through the holes) by doing a running stitch around the design.

Rekindle your love of the nature table by letting your child bring home treasures from their explorations in the garden or on walks. Pine cones, feathers, coins and small plastic toys can be put out on a tray and added to, played with or chatted about. Paying attention to the seasons, the Moon's changing shape, and today's weather are all interesting for children.

At home we have four Bramble Hedge china plates depicting the seasons that Nell found and paid for at a car boot sale. Every quarter the appropriate plate is taken from the cupboard and put on display as a way of keeping a note of the seasons. It would be a shame if they were dropped and smashed beyond repair (they'd become drainage crocks for a potted plant then) but it wouldn't be a disaster. Maybe it would help us dream up a new way to welcome each season – perhaps a song or performance, a candlelit meal or a toast to the fairies?

Offering freedom

It is fairer on children to put breakables out of their reach. But they do need to learn how to stop doing something because it's annoying or dangerous. The trick is to reward good behaviour with attention and praise, but to ignore their attention seeking or bad behaviour. Our tendency towards overprotection means that we sometimes stop our children from learning in the fear that they could be unsafe. Teaching your child to think for herself is an important part of green parenting.

The strange thing about children is that once the umbilical cord is cut parents slowly have to learn to let go as they set about raising a child who will be resilient and adaptable enough to cope with the big changes climate change looks set to bring, including adapting to a low-carbon economy. You can still create nature tables and play I-Spy butterflies but you should also try to let your child and their friends learn to think up solutions to problems because they've seen you have a go and know it's to be encouraged.

It's not only children who will learn from your example. I was really inspired by a woman who lived not so far from me and had a son about six months older than my first daughter. She shared some of the childcare with her partner, was in the first stages of a community project that has gone on to be real success and had a flat that didn't seem to be full of useless gadgets. Her baby slept with his parents, the stairs didn't have a gate at top or bottom (once he could crawl he'd been taught to slither down the stairs safely) and the kitchen was full of fresh produce, not purpose-bought kiddy food. Julie never told me what to do, but watching her taught me to question what I was doing. Was I spooning food into my child's mouth because I'd seen others do that or because it was the best way to feed my daughter (this was before I knew about baby-led weaning)? Did I think I needed a steriliser because all new parents had one? Julie was also an unfussy mum, teaching independence from an early age, a very typical quality of green parents but one that many of us have to consciously force ourselves to learn.

> I never said "be careful, you might fall" or the equivalent when they were exploring or doing active things. It only makes children over-conscious and far less brave, and distracts their attention from what they are doing. One sees so many parents pandering to kids. It's far easier to let them try out what they want, otherwise they never develop co-ordination and judgement.
>
> Anna, 68, anthropologist and mum of Gemma, 31, and Daniel, 28

Sharing childcare

> I have recently started sending my two-year-old to a playgroup for a couple of afternoons and this has given me a couple of hours in the day. I also share childcare with a friend who has a child of a similar age so that we each get every other Wednesday morning off. It's brilliant.
>
> Jo, 39, with Ben, five, and Sally, two

If you are finding it difficult shifting from working girl to mum, remember that you don't have to do the baby care thing every day. The simplest way of occasionally giving yourself a break is to accept help from friends and family. As you get more confident looking after a baby you could try swapping with another mum with a similar-aged child for a couple of hours one or two days a week. This will give you a regular chunk of time on your own to catch up on emails, make dinner, swim or join a yoga class or catch up on sleep. See more on this in chapter 7.

Saturday in the West Country

CASE STUDY

Kathryn, 37, is a mum of three who is a huge fan of babysitting circles (see more in chapter 7). Right now she is keen to get one of her two daughters-in-nappies out of them so is focusing on potty training. Like many couples in charge of kids, the family splits up for some of the day to make childcare easier. The advantage is that you and at least one child enjoy one-on-one time together.

'Today is a Saturday so we are all at home having a lazy morning. It is day two of potty training Mae, two, which was not very successful yesterday as she wanted to go back into nappies. Mae and Alice (four months) are off to a birthday party this afternoon with Daddy and I have given him instructions to take the potty with him! Rosa, five, and I, are off to a school jumble sale to scour for bargains. It's very green to reuse clothes and toys although Rosa did ask if she might be able to buy a Nintendo DS there!'

To look after two or three toddlers for a regular shared childcare date or if your nursery has an inset date make a list of things you can do and stick it up for inspiration. You may be able to do other tasks while the children are busy playing, but be ready to step in and help them whenever it is needed. Lots of mums like getting their kids to help do the cooking. There's less mess if you can kit toddlers out in aprons or put a loose fitting T-shirt that you don't mind getting dirty on top of their outfit.

'Plan activities, such as making gingerbread. Even toddlers can have a go making their dinner. Often I make a pizza base and get them to decorate it themselves (with mushrooms, sweetcorn, etc.). You can buy ready-made bases too. Confetti rice is also a winner: brown rice with lots of raw finely chopped vegetables such as cucumber, tomatoes and peppers.'
Caroline, 33, with Madeleine, six, and Rudy, four

I like using a theme for a long session of toddler care – so I might pretend we are going on a journey. Then I'd find a big cardboard box and get the children to pretend they are canoe-ing or sailing to a treasure island. They should go through a lot of storms and rough seas. Singing 'sea shanties' ('Row Row Row Your Boat' is a good one) adds to the fun. If you've got a dressing-up box then let them dress up as pirates, or be attacked by pirates and then, when everyone's made peace, the pirates can go and feed the ducks at the nearest park or go for a little walk to find the perfect pirate stick.

If you need toddlers in your care to calm down get them to draw, paint or make a model (or colour the outline of some-thing you've drawn) which they can take home to show their family what they spent the day doing. Or if everyone's flagging switch to a quiet story session or provide a snack/meal.

> I like free entertainment – my friends and I tend to live in the skate park/playground in the good weather, taking picnics and hanging out together.

Becky, 37, with Emile, four, and Celeste, five months

As your children move towards their third birthday, going-home time can be a real flash point because most children will not want to stop enjoying themselves. Outrageous. You can try giving your children a ten- or five-minute warning that you will have to leave very soon, but as time is such a vague concept to toddlers it may not work well. You can try lures such as Granny's home or telling them that the goldfish are looking forward to seeing them. Or make sure that your child knows that if she leaves well – having said goodbye and thank you and not resisted putting on her shoes and coat – she will get the chance to spend a long time balancing on the wall you normally rush by. There's no easy way and many children continue to make partings impossible for picker-uppers in a rush.

On long play dates adults need to be contactable at all times, in case of emergencies. You can take it in turns to provide a snack or pack a lunch box.

Provide enough dry clothes/shoes and suitable clothes for playing and going out. Remember that little children get distracted by games so are more likely to wet themselves or get a bit too wet when enjoying water play, so extra leggings, trousers or tights will help make their day more comfortable. Detouring via a second-hand shop is another solution. For a short while it may also be useful to borrow extra equipment for your home – two high chairs, two sets of wellies and a double buggy. If you are willing to let children come on sleep-overs you could try finding a suitable bed on eBay – you can limit your search to a radius of ten miles if you want to save money by sourcing local goods.

Going out of the house

> I thoroughly enjoy being with Jess. I've calmed down now and don't go to all the parent and child classes [singing, baby massage, colour strings, etc.]. I lead a more normal life so go to the shops, the postbox or the park. Going to a class gives a focal point to the day but I only go if I really like the class. Jess likes being outside really.
>
> Jo, 42, with Jess, 20 months

Little babies are light enough to carry around easily. As you recover from the birth you will get stronger too which means you could find a sling/backpack useful right up to your baby's second birthday, and maybe longer. But it's the first months when they are particularly suited for baby wearing. Using a sling allows you to go anywhere or do anything with your baby, including chores like washing up and vacuuming. You could go to a trendy baby sign class, an art gallery, visit a friend, try a Mum and Baby cinema show, go to the library or enjoy a walk. What you are doing may not seem particularly green, but by getting your child involved in every part of your life you are setting yourself up to find childcare a much less stressful experience.

> I'm not sure that at this age there are very green choices available – we just go to the local mother and

baby groups, and chat to other mothers. I reckon green activities will come later. We do the occasional nature walk, with the vague idea that it might instil an appreciation of the outdoors, but I'm not sure I'd classify that as "green".
Jess, 39, with Connie, six months

Many councils offer a list of places in the borough or county that are eco-noteworthy from Green Flag parks to eco-demo and Energy Advice centres. Have you actually seen a green roof yet or a living wall or a wildflower meadow?

How about setting yourself the target of getting to know the interesting eco-things that are happening in your neighbourhood? Canals, rivers, woodlands and allotments offer opportunities for games, wildlife spotting and a chance to connect with the seasons. You can do something similar in very urban areas – just look at the street tree pits, front gardens and any verges to find dandelions, shepherd's purse and interesting bugs.

Be prepared when out and about. I always made sure, and indeed still make sure, that I have healthy snacks such as fruit, healthy cereal bars (not the ones packed with sugars), fruit "leathers", etc. And we got into healthy habits – with a fruit snack when we got home. It's fantastic when your child actually requests a fruit snack.
Sharon, 40, with Saffron, nine

To stay out longer, stock up on the right kind of clothing and pack snacks. For a six-month-plus baby take water and fruit, raisins, cold boiled/baked potatoes or bread as well as rice cakes or bread sticks to keep your child's energy levels up between meals. A baby and a breastfeeding mum are both allowed to snack, and because you know your child, you will know when they are hungry.

There are also some amazing day trips to be had from anyone's house, especially if you live near a train station or bus stop. If you live in Teesside you've got beaches, moors and ruined abbeys. If you live in Stroud you've got the Cotswolds. In London you are spoilt by the number of rail routes that can whisk you away. Dry autumn days and not too hot summer weather, when the daylight is long and the weather clement, are brilliant for longer trips with a baby. Using train and bus services, I enjoyed big days out as a first-time mum at the National Fruit Collection at Brogdale with its 3,500 varieties of apples, pears and plums; I looked around vineyards in Kent and in Bedfordshire visited woodlands managed for coppice, cutting and wildlife. But mostly I learnt to dawdle in the area close to where I live and I found the baby, invariably strapped to me, would enjoy what I enjoyed because she felt involved in an interesting life.

An afternoon walk with Jago, two years and eight months

CASE STUDY

Jago's mum is pregnant and desperate for some quiet time to catch up with emails and take a rest. He's my nephew so taking my daughters (eight and ten) we go out for a family walk in the Hertfordshire countryside. All the children are wearing wellies. I've got bananas for a halfway snack and emergency raisins, which two-year-olds usually love and older children enjoy too.

Jago's mum says he's a good walker and likes the short trips to post a letter, buy eggs from a neighbour's gate or look at horses grazing in a field. We take the dog on a lead too who will provide all of us with excitement as she sniffs for rabbits and scans the route for other walkers. It's a warm spring afternoon enlivened by chiff-chaff, the first sightings of orange tip butterflies and our route through a scented bluebell wood. We play all sorts of games, including splash in the puddles, race the cousins, play catch tag, spot wildlife at welly-boot height (a spider on a bluebell, a white deadnettle), look for rabbits in the middle distance, smell what Ted Hughes called 'the sudden sharp hot stink of fox' (from 'The Thought Fox'), say hello to other dog walkers, chat about Jago's interests (mostly pirates and snacks at the moment), tell stories and sing a lot of marching songs to keep everyone going.

Happy outside

Have you heard about forest schools? They originated in Scandinavia, where the children seem to be born in thermal underwear and all-in-one waterproofs. It's all about "there is no such thing as bad weather, only bad clothing". So get wrapped up, put hot food or stew in your thermos flask and get out there. Once you have the muddy puddles outfit – then everything else is free – assuming that you have a bit of muddy woodland close by.
Lucy, 44, with Natalie, six, and Isis, three

Whizzing a child around in a buggy isn't ideal once your child wants to practise walking. Those early walking months are a time to enjoy going very slowly as you let your child explore parks, pavements, verges and the joys of look and touch. There will be plenty of times when your toddler refuses to go any further by foot: fair enough if they are worn out or hungry. But you can sometimes trick them into walking for longer with

Tip

Here's some others games to play:

- ◯ Chasing
- ◯ Walking like a mouse (or elephant or tiger)
- ◯ See if you can reach that flower before me
- ◯ Avoiding cracks in the pavement
- ◯ Shadow jumping
- ◯ Balancing along low walls
- ◯ Hopping and skipping
- ◯ Running games (downhill, to the next but one tree)
- ◯ Find something blue and wait for me there
- ◯ Pick up red leaves, rubber bands, twigs, pebbles, petals
- ◯ Look for an ant or a hoverfly
- ◯ Find a good place for a picnic
- ◯ Find a house with Christmas lights
- ◯ Look for people in hats
- ◯ Tell me which way to go to get home
- ◯ Listen for a bird or a mobile phone ringtone
- ◯ Make a wish when you see a walker in a red coat
- ◯ Let your toddler choose a stick to carry home
- ◯ Anything else you can think of!

games. If you've read the wonderful *We're Going on a Bear Hunt* by Children's Laureate Michael Rosen, then you will know how to encourage your child through gloopy mud, swishy grass, splashy water, etc.

The pay-off for getting your toddler to walk more (besides making them fit and developing good exercise habits) is that he will be hungry enough to eat the food you've prepared and maybe sleep better too. Fingers crossed.

Even toddlers can enjoy walks that are all about playing. Let them toddle if they are walking until they tire and then pop them in a sling rather than pushing a cumbersome buggy along the route too. And if your child doesn't need the sling you can always use it to scrump crab apples, heap up black-berries and rosehips or harvest the first spring nettles. The secret to a really enjoyable walk is to go slowly: let the children explore and follow their ideas for play. And don't forget to bring snacks and tap water because children need regular rests and refuelling.

'Going on a walk with a group is more fun. Everyone gets to see how we "parent" our children and learn from each other, also people bring along such interesting picnic food to share including rice cakes, Brazil nuts, Philadelphia cheese, ham wraps and tinned rice pudding. It's much easier to chat to people walking rather than sitting face-to-face inside. If you are out in high summer paddling in streams is always good. Let your toddlers' wellies fill up with water! Let them get wet splashing. They mind much less than we do. '

Rachel, 44, outdoor play leader, with George, 11, Tobias, nine, Arthur, six. See www. playingoutdoors.co.uk.

And if you can't go on a walk you can always bring the outside inside by bringing piles of natural materials to the places children play. All ages can enjoy games with feathers, earth, sticks, willow cuttings, non-poisonous leaves and berries, hazel, gravel and sheep's wool. One play centre in Bath has regular deliveries of natural materials for the children to enjoy using in their games.

If there's something you love doing, but maybe didn't have the time when you were working, now might be the time to splash out on an annual pass so you can regularly visit a place in all seasons. Arboretums, zoos, London's Historic Royal Palaces, National Trust, English Heritage or places more local to you usually offer good value annual passes. They are expensive one-off buys, but if you can make child care feel like a holiday or a good chance to learn then it's a more than justifiable expense. Besides, it's hard to go proper shopping with a baby so you should find your clothes bill slashed (not to mention the after-work wine-bar tab).

Baby steps

Small

○ Sing more to your baby (lullabies, nursery rhymes, pop songs).
○ Resist all educational toys – they are appealing to your pushy mum side but they cost, often have batteries and will clutter your home. Instead make your own treasure basket.
○ Make your garden child friendly. Add some small dishes to collect treasures, plants, etc. You don't have to have grand ambitions, just think how your child's curiosity could be satisfied without having to trek to the park.

Medium

○ Find a local mum to show you what's happening locally that's suitable for you and/or the age of your child. Pin up a list of things you can do with a baby/toddler/more than one little child in case you need inspiration.

○ Even if it's raining you can go to the park – you can have fun sheltering, or listening to rain drops on the buggy. cover/umbrella. Splashing in puddles is always entertaining. In the autumn let them kick leaves, search for conkers, hazel cobs and prickly sweet chestnuts. Stock up on waterproof gear, fleeces and wellies so you can stay out longer.

○ Organise a more ambitious trip to somewhere you really want to go and you think the baby/child would enjoy too. Can you get there by public transport?

Large

○ Notice the state of public playgrounds and parks – do they need a clean up, can you help by writing to a councillor, picking up litter, organising a tidy-up, getting recycling bins put in?

○ Let your child explore and try things out for himself/herself much more. Babies are programmed to do this, it's you who is going to have to learn not to interfere.

○ Try sharing childcare for short spells.

Seven

Sleeping, Baths and No-Fee Babysitting

How much – and where – your baby sleeps will be fundamental to your sanity, energy levels and ability to be a creative parent. Make this time easier for yourself by taking your baby with you when you go out (and go out earlier). Also find out how you can join or set up a babysitting circle made up of local families.

Sleeping

The big sleep debate is a cultural obsession – entirely appropriate for a 24/7 society. Last night's insomnia is something to talk about if you've exhausted the weather. And for parents of young children, sleep – or the lack of it – is even more of a hot topic.

There isn't a green way to send your baby to sleep. Where they sleep (with you, near you or somewhere else); what you buy in terms of equipment and how you deal with crying are matters for individual families to sort out. If you can't function without sleep, if your relationship with your partner is becoming strained through sheer lack of sleep or you have to go back to a demanding job when your baby is still only able to digest breast milk or formula, then just follow the nighttime routine that allows you to cope best.

Families with older children often haven't cracked the sleep conundrum, either. It's not unusual to have to lie down in the early evening with a toddler in an attempt to trick them into sleeping. The problem is that it's too easy to fall asleep in a cosy, dark room beside your cute sleepy child, wrecking your evening plans. While it's nice falling asleep like this, what's not so nice is when you think your little one has nodded off and you creep to the door and suddenly there's a big shout of 'Where are you going?' And so you start the whole process again...

Sleep consolation

There are consolations for being awake when the world's asleep – seeing moonlight cross the room, listening to your family's contented sleepy breathing or watching urban fox cubs take turns to bound up a blanketed car and then slide down the bonnet. Listening to owls, foxes and muntjac barking in the dark, or picking out the birds of the dawn chorus (thrush, robin, wren). I was awake so much during my babies' early lives that I hardly missed anything they did.

During one lunchtime my boss and I counted up the number of hours we'd tried to get our similarly aged children to bed and reckoned that we'd lost over a year coaxing infants to sleep. It was sobering to think how anarchistic our children were about time.

Where will your baby sleep?

Item	Advantages	Disadvantages	Tips
New or second-hand Moses basket near your bed	Portable, lots around	Quickly outgrown, often hard to clean	
In a drawer (removed from chest of drawers) and put near your bed	Portable, already in your home, easy to clean	May seem eccentric but is an eco-friendly and cheap option used by many	
Cot and baby sleeping bags	Bedding stays on child. You can make your own	Quickly outgrown, need at least two in case your child is sick or nappy leaks (or just switch to sheet/blankets and warm night-clothes)	Ask other parents how they handled washing arrangements, etc.
Co-sleeping with baby in three-sided cot next to big bed, or shares a family bed with parents	Cosy for child, easiest way to offer nighttime feeding on demand. Possible from day one	Not suitable if adult under influence of alcohol, medication or other drugs. Bad if nappy leaks. Be alert to FSID risks	Put a plastic mattress protector on to bed. Lay baby on towel or use biodegradable disposable nappy

What sleep kit does my baby need?

Cots: It's easy to find a second-hand cot in good condition. If a friend or family member hasn't passed you one then you'll find what you want in NCT sales and on eBay. If you give yourself time before your baby arrives, or are willing to do some paint repairs, Freecycle is another good option.

Bedding: Cot-sized sheets and blankets can be made by cutting any spare sheets to fit. This isn't a very skilled job, but if you can't sew, and no one you know can be persuaded to help, ask at a dry cleaner's or launderette.

Sleeping bags: Sleeping bags are a personal duvet for your child – shop ones fasten like dungarees on the shoulder, and may have a zip at the side too. You will need the right weight for the season and your house's temperature, and have one on, one in the wash, and a spare, just to be on the safe side, and all have to be the right size – this makes them quite expensive. On the plus side they make some things simple: if your child is in a cot, for instance, you can lift them warmly out of

DIY baby sleeping bag

To cut back on your expenses, either look for pre-loved baby sleeping bags or make your own. A simple version is to sew fleecy material or a portion of a blanket together in a rectangular pillow case shape and pop your baby into that (you don't even need to add dungaree fastenings at the shoulder). Try teaming up with crafty friends and see if you can run them up together, stitch and bitch style.

bed to breastfeed and then pop them back without having to fuss over bedding.

Night light (or not): It's much easier to feed a baby if your room isn't really dark. If you live in a home with street lighting nearby, then you may get enough light in the winter by leaving a gap in your curtains. Or you could leave a light with an energy-efficient light bulb in it on in the corridor or an adjacent room. Plug in night lights may seem useful, however a child put to bed with a night light will find it hard to adjust to rooms without them.

Black-out curtains (or not): Material that doesn't let the moon, streetlights, car lights or dawn brighten your baby's bedroom is not expensive to buy and acts as a double lining of your curtains, making your windows leak less heat. Long curtains are also much more fun for games of peekaboo.

You can make your rooms darker by triple-lining curtains (good for energy efficiency too) and being sure that the curtain material generously fits the rail.

Baby monitor (or not): Avoid unless your home is colossal or you or your partner have hearing problems. You can keep doors open so you can hear what's happening, or your toddler can get out of bed and come and tell you. Things get complicated if your second child isn't much older than your first. Do you really want to be listening out for two monitors?

Nightclothes: Not needed during the first year. Just dress in an All-in-one night and day to save you expense and faff. However, a nightie is a good choice, whatever your child's gender, if you anticipate changing nappies at night.

Your own bed: There may be times when your baby falls asleep in your bed, so it makes sense to think how to make being in your bed safe for them – always make sure they can't roll off (see section below on co-sleeping). Some families find that unscrewing the bed legs so that the mattress rests on the floor is the safest option during the baby years – that way neither toddler nor baby will be hurt if they roll off the mattress. For those one-off times when you are staying away from home you could soften any potential falls from a bed by laying out a thick rug or pillows below.

Co-sleeping

'I did sleep with the babies in my bed. People commented that they'd be worried that they would squish the baby or the duvet would suffocate them. But we slept down the bed and the baby at the top. It's much more relaxing because you can feed at night. Your instinct is there, you just won't harm them. I felt it was safer because you can hear every sniffle and snuffle. And it was really nice.'
Tara, 37, with Olivia, ten, Eve, seven, and Orla, four

The woman who made us all think about co-sleeping as a traditional and humane way of parenting is Jean Liedloff. In her fascinating book *Continuum Concept* she details how a South American tribe hold their children close until they are ready to do things themselves – approximately two years of age. The book was written in the 1970s and yet it's still considered a bit freaky by some people to carry a child around, or have your baby in your bed with you.

There's a good reason for this, the concerns about cot death. Each year around 500 babies suffer what's known as cot death but the numbers are hugely reduced since families learnt to avoid smoking in children's rooms/homes and started putting their babies to sleep on their backs. The Foundation for the Study of Infant Deaths (FSID) says that the safest place for your baby to sleep for the first six months of his life is in a cot in the same room as you. FSID warns against sleeping in the same bed (or on the sofa or an armchair) with your baby, especially if the person holding the baby is using drugs, alcohol or is very tired.

My partner was won over to co-sleeping after reading *Babywatching* by Desmond Morris, which made him hate the idea of leaving our baby alone in her own room (or, for that matter, in her cot in the corner) all night. Infants are so animal-like, and most young animals (think puppies and kittens here) like being in a pack cuddled up safe and close to their mum and siblings. I suspect that being left in a dark, hushed room must make a suddenly waking baby instinctively fear that everyone's died. No wonder they wail, and how sad that so many women still follow advice they hate to leave their child crying.

How you co-sleep is up to your family and the amount of space you have. You can share your bed with your baby or if this just isn't wide enough you can put the baby to sleep in a three-sided cot beside the bed. The bed and cot mattresses will both need to be the same height, and the baby must not be able to fall into a gap between the beds, or between your bed's mattress and the headboard.

The advantages of co-sleeping are that your baby will cry for less time during the night because you are close enough to feed her as soon as she wakes. In fact, she may not even cry but just nuzzle up to you for milk. You will also be able to take her wherever you want to go without any extra equipment. You'll also be able to share one bed for some time, which will reduce the amount of furniture needed in your home. Your baby will probably be ready for her own bed at two and a bit.

How to co-sleep in comfort and safety

If you co-sleep, or ever bring your baby into the bed for nighttime breastfeeding (the obvious place in a cold winter house at night) you should not be drunk, drugged or unwell.

○ Lie your baby between adults or between an adult and the wall so that he cannot roll out.

○ Beware suffocation. You can use pillows or rolled-up towels to keep your baby wedged in a safe spot at the top end of the bed. Falling out is dangerous and if you are tired mistakes can easily happen.

○ Prevent your baby overheating or suffocating if he wriggles under heavy blankets or a duvet by having their head much nearer the bed head than your own. You don't need an extra wide (or even long) bed, just divide the pillows so there is a canyon where the baby can lie flat. That way their eye level will be about the same as any sleeping adult's.

○ Prevent disaster from sick or nappies leaking on to bedclothes by putting your child to sleep on a waterproof mat or a double folded towel. Also use a mattress cover.

Books with a message

Children love story time and may continue to enjoy listening to a family book at bedtime even in their teens. The popularity of Radio 4's *Book at Bedtime* suggests lots of us crave a nighttime story.

○ Let your baby hold the book, chewing may happen so board books make sense. Don't let that put you off a second-hand copy. See what looks popular at the library and then take it out.

○ Barefoot Books produces colourfully illustrated stories, often with international themes. They offer the opportunity for parents to sell books from the Barefoot range, thus giving them the opportunity to make money. See www.barefootbooks.com.

Bathing

For me bath time is play, it's fun in the water not for getting clean. My children have a bath every other night and all five of us use the same bath water. When they were babies I always had a bath with the baby – just add a drop of lavender oil and it knocks them out for a blissful sleep.

Tara, 37, with Olivia, ten, Eve, seven, and Orla, four

It should be a human right to have clean water, healthy food and unpolluted air. But unwittingly many of us use cleaning products and cosmetics that spoil our water sources and pollute the air quality, indoors and out. The reality is that you don't need to use anything more than warm water on your baby. And if his skin becomes dry then organic olive oil is the perfect moisturiser.

Most baths need 80 litres of water run, although you probably won't be running it so deep for little children. Baths waste your expensive energy too; unless you've got solar thermal installed you will also have to keep using oil/gas, even during the summer, to keep your water hot.

Reusing bath water is one option. And when the water is cold you can also use a siphon or buckets to decant some of the water for use on plants or young trees although it is likely to be less effort to save for flushing the loo. Given each bath's environmental footprint, it makes sense to use them as a treat rather than an everyday necessity – unless that's your special time with the kids.

Read the labels

Few women – and a growing number of men – can resist the pleasures of creams and scented products. But could we be creating a chemical cocktail that is wrecking our health? With milk ducts close to the places you apply antiperspirant, breasts submerged under scented bubble baths and perfume or aftershave applied close to where your baby is carried and cuddled, it's no wonder lots of people are starting to wonder just how damaging the products listed on the labels are for their young children. While the jury remains out, there are some ingredients to avoid:

○ Parabens are preservatives. Do you want to put creams on your child that have a shelf life that could keep them fresh for years?

- Parfum is the blanket term for more than 2,500 fragrances, of which 24 are known to be common triggers for allergic reactions.
- Phthalates help make plastic flexible so you can find them in rubber ducks (and many other children's toys), shower curtains, shop bought plastic water bottles and nail varnish. These plasticisers will leach if damaged (so don't reuse your water bottles, buy a proper water container from a camping store) and are known to feminise male fish. There are concerns over whether they are feminising human males too.
- Sodium laurel sulphate is a powerful cleaning agent – the more in the product, the more corrosive it is.

For mums who wear lippy, there's a thrifty answer for your make-up bag. Don't give up the products you enjoy, just use less. Try using a smidgeon of shampoo rather than a dollop. Be sparing with bath oils, suncream and face creams. Try spraying perfume on to your clothes rather than directly on to your skin.

Unless a baby's hair gets dirty (perhaps with food or sick), there is no need to wash with shampoo. The time to start lathering is if they should get head lice (very common) or when they become old enough to sweat.

Potion and lotion ideas

- You could try mixing your own beauty creams as there are many courses available, or you could have a go on your own or with friends. Once you've been on a course you are sure to end up sharing the magic by presenting your friends with little gifts you've whipped up in your home apothecary. Your children can learn a lot from seeing DIY beauty creams created too.

○ If you can't afford organic olive oil (or would rather use this for drizzling across salads) then buy the cheaper, blended oils on any dry skin.

○ Create your own macerated products by soaking a plant in a mix of water and alcohol for two weeks and then pressing the tincture out.

○ Try supporting a UK industry – like Norfolk lavender; or choose potions that are grown in the UK – such as the organic herbs used in Neal's Yard remedies or Napier's mixes, or try out the biodynamic grown products produced by Weleda, www.weleda.com.

○ Organically certified brands are listed at the Soil Association's health and beauty pages. Many of these products have loyal fans, but they do not get the same exposure than the more conventional products, who are backed up by the multimillion-pound cosmetics industry.

○ Take a washed, laddered pair of tights/stockings then cut into 10-cm lengths. Stuff with a cup of oats and seal with a knot. Throw under running warm water to make a moisturising bath. After the bath compost the oats (or feed to a pet/add to bird feeders) and either bin or wash then recycle the tights. If you add a pretty ribbon this can even be a gift.

○ If you are looking for ideas try *Green Parent*, *Resurgence*, www.theecologist.org and eco sections of mainstream women's, beauty/health and lifestyle magazines.

Some children love their evening bath, and it can also be special for a working parent too, as they can really enjoy playing and bonding with their child as you both wind down before bed. Bath times are great for singing songs and splashing practice. Little children really love bath toys too – a floating wooden spoon, a cork that bobs and shell that keeps sinking will provide early scientific experiments. What will a leaf, a milk top and a model polar bear do?

Tonight at home with... CASE STUDY

Elaine is a community activist who specialises in environmental justice. She is on maternity leave and her partner works from home a few days a week. They've been making their home more energy efficient, and now also have a very young baby, so Elaine's mum has come to stay. Here's last night's bedtime for Finn (two and a half) and two-week-old brother, Niall.

6 p.m.: Teatime. Mum, Dad, Nanny, Finn and Niall (asleep). Finn has just discovered the delight of eating spaghetti strand by strand.

6.40 p.m.: *Charlie and Lola* time: highlight of the day. Mum and Finn watch the DVD, with Finn armed with a bowl of grapes and strawberries.

7.15 p.m.: Finn's milk time and play time with Dad – normally either a jigsaw or trains and track.

7.45 p.m.: Finn and Mum read books.

8 p.m.: Finn and Dad have a bath together.

8.15–8.30 p.m.: Dad puts Finn to bed (in his own room, where he and his parents all slept until he was two years old). Finn has a full-sized single bed now.

9.30 p.m. Elaine goes to bed, taking Niall with her. At 11 p.m. Dad changes Niall's nappy and gives a bottle of expressed breast milk to him. He has a feed at 2 a.m. and 5 a.m. and wakes again at 7 a.m. It's like this for the next eight weeks.

Three months on Niall goes to bed at 7 p.m. and has breast milk from Mum at 10 p.m., 1 a.m., 4 a.m. and 6 a.m.

Babysitting

Just because you're a parent doesn't mean you have to be confined to the house. It also doesn't need to be prohibitively expensive. With a bit of imagination you can soon develop a network of friends and family who will share looking after each other's children. There are so many options available that you need not be stuck at home.

Take the baby with you

You can take a little baby almost anywhere – from festivals to restaurants. If you are into meals and can afford it, you could always go out at lunchtime when many restaurants offer special deals. Towards the end of their first year when babies start being able to crawl it becomes awkward to bring them to some grown-up venues.

> I make time to attend training and events for the issues I care about – this wouldn't be possible without an understanding and supportive husband. So I go to Greenpeace meetings in the evenings and have

started a Transition Town group. I spend about three
evenings a week devoted to my environmental
projects.

,

Jo, 39, with Ben, five, and Sally, two

New parents often take it in turns to stay at home minding the baby, while the other does something they want to do. However much you want company when your baby has gone to bed, it's worth being considerate about your partner's occasional need to go to the pub quiz, go out with colleagues or whatever it is they're pining for – just be sympathetic to your other half, and make sure that you get to do the things you love too.

Baby stays at home

If you have adopted a bedtime routine that you don't want to break, or your baby is unlikely to be calm at a restaurant or pub, you need to think up different ways to go out. Obviously, it is illegal to leave babies at home on their own but you might manage a matinee or early evening film if you've got a sensible 16-year-old at home who can look after a much younger sibling or you could use a babysitter. The NSPCC recommends that babysitters should be a minimum age of 16. Finding a babysitter and organising occasional or regular slots for them to mind your sleeping kids is brilliant, but for families who are working part-time or have just one salary it may be only practical as an occasional treat.

You will probably need childcare (especially at night) until your oldest child is 14 years old, although this is a personal decision. Considering that conventional babysitting is at least a fiver an hour, and will be much more in cities (near me the rate is £8 an hour), and factoring in the need to escort, drop off or pay for a taxi to get your babysitter home, it is obvious that finding alternatives to a not very experienced teenager babysitter will save you a small fortune – and peace of mind.

Babysitting rules

- ○ Swap mobile numbers.
- ○ Make sure your babysitter knows what time you'd like your children to be in bed (if they aren't in bed already), and if there is a time they must stop reading or talking.
- ○ Leave out any medication (asthma reliever, cough lozenges).
- ○ Tell them when you are due back, and agree the hourly rate you will pay before you go out (pay double time after midnight).
- ○ If it's winter and cold you may need to keep your heating on for longer than usual, or show where the blankets are located or check they know how to use your type of heating system.
- ○ Lay out some snacks, be clear about what they can eat or drink. Give info about your wi-fi/broadband connection.
- ○ Leave the house quickly with no fuss.

No-fee babysitting

We do babysitting swaps with a close friends – first Friday of the month they sit for us, third Friday we sit for them. It works because we are all really keen to get out. It's really nice because you know you are going to have a babysitter so you get around to organising something. And it feels completely fair. I like having a babysitter who knows the children, so then they can read them a story and get them into bed. **9**

Anna, 36, with Freddie, four, and Elsie, two

Many families make use of a grandparent to have a break. But as many women now often have their first child in their thirties it means that their own parents may not be fit enough to cope with the demands of a baby or toddler or live too far away.

The alternative is swapping babysitting nights with another family that guarantee the grown-ups in your house get a night out at least once a month, or give you some regular private time to go back to your kick-boxing class, or whatever you did before becoming a parent.

Babysitting swaps

- ○ Let each family take turns, it's best if there's a regular day scheduled, then barb wire it into the diary for the next three months (or more).
- ○ Don't be too ambitious, this is a once or twice a month activity.
- ○ Don't change dates unless you really have to, or if both families are very flexible.
- ○ If you usually pick a weekday be sensitive to the other family's work commitments. Check it's okay to be back late.

Babysitting circles

' Joining the babysitting circle has been one of the best things we've done since moving here. It has made going out so much more affordable. It's also helped us to hold on to some part of the social life we had before our girls came along. As our girls know all the mums and dads in the circle, we don't feel uneasy about leaving them with these adults and, as every member is a parent themselves, we don't have to explain what to do. '

Kathryn, with Rosa, seven, Mae, two, and Alice, five months

A babysitting circle draws on a bigger pool of families for childcare than a swap system. It is composed of a group of families with young children who are happy to babysit for the other members and are willing to ask members to babysit when they want to go out. Each time a person babysits they earn tokens, with extra tokens earned for Saturday nights and each hour after midnight. Most babysitting circles are restricted to couples – this is because the set-up is usually that one person looks after their own children at home while their partner looks after the babysitting family's children at their home. This is infuriating for single parents, but every circle is different, so ask. And as relationships change the opportunity to be on a babysitting circle list can open as fast as it closes.

Babysitting circles seem to work best if one person coor-dinates updating the families on the list and the collecting/ distributing of tokens to joining and quitting families. Eight families will be rather small for a circle, but with 10 to 14 on the list, it can operate brilliantly.

When you join an existing circle you should receive a list of all member families with details of their children's names and some starter tokens. These tokens can be exchanged for babysitting hours (which are usually measured in half-hours).

Sample babysitting token schemes

	Scheme 1 (London)	Scheme 2 (Bath)
How many tokens do you get on joining?	18 tokens	20 tokens
How much for half an hour of babysitting?	1 token	1 token
What if it's after 11 p.m.?	2 tokens per half-hour after 11 p.m.	See below
What if it is before 6 p.m. or after midnight?	See above	2 tokens per half-hour before 6 p.m. or from midnight
What if it is a Friday?	1 extra token	n/a
What's the cost in tokens of going out on Saturday from 8–11.30 p.m.?	8–11 is three hours, so 6 tokens. The last half-hour costs 2 tokens. Total 8 tokens	8–11.30 is three and a half hours, so total is 7 tokens

Ninety per cent of the time the system has worked for us. Sometimes we can owe, or be owed, tokens, but this is rare. The only problem is that many of us in the circle socialise together so there can be some occasions when most of us are invited to the same event. However, our treasurer has recently organised a Christmas get-together for all parents and children which was a good way to get to know new families and children.

Kathryn, 37, with Rosa, seven, Mae, two, and Alice, five months

The babysitting circle my family uses – which has been established for long enough to have had more than 50 families over 15 years on the scheme – uses handmade laminated tokens. When you are invited to join you are given the rules and 18 tokens. When you leave you give back 18 tokens.

Tips for babysitting circles

○ If you are setting one up don't feel restricted to asking only like-minded families. What you need are responsible couples, with babies and primary school-aged children, who like going out.

○ Use it – go out or babysit each week/fortnight (maybe on a regular day so you don't forget).

○ Keep your tokens safe – you have to hand over the same number you started with before you can quit the scheme.

○ Get to know the other members so you feel confident about them looking after your children, and so that they feel the same about you looking after their kids.

Sleepovers

It takes more organising when children are little, but you could also arrange for your toddler to have an occasional sleepover with a friend. Sleepovers work best if your child knows the host family well and knows what to expect.

Tips for sleepovers

Not all two-year-olds will be mature enough to cope with a sleepover, but if they are up for it, here's how:

○ Put your child's clothes in a roomy bag so it's easy to pack up in the morning before they leave their friend's home. Don't forget their PJs and cuddly toy (and any nighttime nappy needs).

○ Leave your number and any medication.

○ Let the host family know what time and how your child normally goes to sleep – with the door open and a light in the corridor, for instance.

○ You can save the host family having to wash bed linen by getting your child to take along their own sleeping bag (or travel cot). Or take along a pillowcase and a duvet cover which can be used as a bed liner, again saving on laundry chores.

Baby steps

Small

○ Decide how you'd like to look after your baby at nighttime – as a co-sleeper or not – and then aim to be uncritical of any other methods.

○ Make your own spare cot sheets and blanketing from the excess in your linen drawer.

○ If you are using disposable nappies switch to a biodegradable brand for nighttime.

Medium

○ Consider using a baby sleeping bag if you are worried about your child kicking off their blankets. You could even make your own.

○ Organise a babysitting swap night.

○ Get your name down on a babysitting circle if there's one locally, as there can be a long wait.

Large

○ Turn your room into a safe place for family sleeping.

○ Set up a babysitting circle if it doesn't exist locally, or offer to host one of the annual babysitting gatherings so you get to meet more families who want to go out.

○ Start using your free time in the evening for something that inspires you.

Eight
Getting Around

Buggies may signal 'parent of young child' in the UK but for most of the world the sling's the thing because it is comfy, cheap and keeps your baby a heartbeat away from their carer. In this chapter find out how to fit two or three on a bike, repair a buggy, all the ways to get the best trips on public transport and join a car club.

Cars – especially if you already have one – offer all sorts of conveniences for longer trips, but with a baby you may find that having a variety of ways of getting around is more efficient, and fun.

Slings

> It would not be a bad idea, as long as there are so many prams in the world, to put the shopping in them and carry the baby.
>
> Jean Liedloff, The Continuum Concept

Wearing your baby in a sling is quintessential green parenting. Slings are incredibly practical if you have to look after a baby and do most things yourself, not just baby care but household chores and even gardening. Most babies settle well because they are close to their parent and take comfort in being back in that womblike position soothed by a nearby heartbeat.

> If I only could have two things I'd want a sling for carrying the baby outside and indoors so you can get on with other things you have to do. There are lots of online sling shops and you can also get them via UK Babywearing Swap, a yahoo group for buying and selling second-hand slings, or from eBay. You can also get good advice at slingmeet.co.uk and its local groups. And then, it depends. If you travel by car, a car seat!
>
> Rachel, 39, with Leila, four, and Ravi, 17 months

Slings are far easier to store, and much cheaper than a buggy. You can use an adjustable piece of cloth, a sarong or buy one with loads of clicks and straps. Try your sling out with a doll first, then once the real baby is inside get out of the house because a walking pace settles a baby. If you're uncomfortable, stop another baby-wearer to check you've fitted it right or take photos of the way you are wearing it and then compare with the manufacturer's suggested position. If you don't get on with a sling, don't worry as for most of us it is only a two-year phase and may be much shorter depending on your baby's desire to practise walking skills and your own strength.

> My wife wants a sling as we don't have an additional car. Wearing the baby in a sling and carrying shopping is much easier on public transport.
>
> Tony, 32, with Jashan, six and a half weeks

Ten reasons why I love using a sling

Jo, 34, whose son Billy is 17 months old, loves her sling so much she still hasn't got a buggy: 'The sling was quite expensive but it's one of the three things I bought – everything else was second-hand or borrowed – that I really recommend to new parents. Besides the Ergo, which cost approximately £90, we couldn't have lived without a three-sided cot that you can put beside your bed to co-sleep, around £180, and a wooden Tripp Trapp high chair for £130, which I hope he'll still be able to use when he's at university as they can be converted into adult seating.'

1. Having your baby in a sling is one big constant cuddle
2. You are hands-free
3. Babies cry less when carried
4. When very young, carrying babies in slings is like an extension of being in the womb – he feel the movements and sounds of mum or dad
5. It keeps you fit and helps you lose your baby weight
6. It promotes strong attachment, which is believed to promote happy, healthy, confident and secure children
7. Your baby isn't on a level with car exhausts when walking along a road
8. Your baby is at the same height as other people, so helps them learn social and language skills as you interact with others
9. Allows you to communicate better with your baby while you're on the move, especially when carrying on the front – you don't have to stoop to tell your baby you love him
10. You can breastfeed on the go (optional!)

As your baby gets heavier you get stronger, so if your child isn't unusually large you should be able to comfortably carry them for six months, but probably much longer. The trick is to hold your stomach muscles in to make sure you use all your core for carrying, not just your back.

I'm a fan of the Baby Bjorn carrier which looks like a pouch and is worn on your front so you can put a light backpack on your back with your keys, purse, a change of clothes, nappies, etc., rather than have to tend to a handbag that's easily forgotten and not so easy to wear. Others rave about the American Ergo carrier, which can be worn front or back. There are also baby backpacks for hiking, which are bulkier to store but have useful waterproof attachments so your baby stays dry in downpours and can be balanced successfully on the ground (like a high chair) when you need a break. You don't have to go off road with these backpacks, a stroll to the shops using a backpack instead of a pushchair can make a nice change.

If you no longer need your sling then pass it on or flog on eBay. One of my friends asked for Lola's outgrown material sling so she could use it to carry her puppy around before his vaccinations were complete. The photos she sent were beguilingly cute – it's enough to make you want your next child to have shaggy hair and soft pointy ears.

Buggies

I can walk for three hours with my baby in the buggy, but I can't do that in the sling. I chose a buggy that has got suspension so I can go along lanes and the canal. I wanted to know it was strong (so I could put shopping underneath it) and well made so it will last, and will probably do for somebody else.

Anne, 43, with Edgar, five months

Most families find that after two or three months' sling wearing they also need an easy-to-fold up buggy. By waiting a few months after your baby's birth you will be able to select exactly

Storing a buggy

' The double buggy makes being out and about without a car so much easier. It has made many journeys possible when otherwise I would have stayed at home. '

Hannah, 34, with Iola, three, and Cai, ten months

Outside – ideally under cover, out of sight, use bike PJs or a waterproof sheet, possibly with a bike lock to secure. Will it fit into a garden shed or your garage or the boot of your car?

Inside – try to fold it up if you don't want your corridor/kitchen/ living room blocked. But some buggies double as high chairs or a place for a daytime sleep so you may prefer not to fold it up. Or can you fold up and hang from somewhere? You can buy strong wall fittings suitable for bikes from cycle shops that can double up as buggy hooks. Do your neighbours mind if it is left in a shared hallway? Can you leave it folded out of sight behind a sofa/opening door? When it's wet avoid wheeling wet pools and mud trails into your home by parking your buggy on a doormat or carpet cut-off. Or put down a piece of cardboard.

the model you think will best suit – and you may even be able to borrow a buggy rather than buy it as people are always trying to offload them in a bid to declutter their homes. Ask around or try Freecycle. You can still use a sling but a buggy gives you somewhere to park your baby when it gets heavier or needs a sleep. And if you buy a robust model then you can load it with your shopping.

If you find that the buggy you want costs more than you would pay for a pair of shoes or a bike, ask yourself if you would be able to park it outside your home, or a café or at a nursery without panicking that it might be stolen. You may feel that fussing about your buggy's whereabouts, or even D-locking it up, is not the sort of habit you want to get into. If that's so, then pick a cheaper model.

' The reason the vast majority of people have those umbrella-style strollers is because they are a very cheap, practical, hard-wearing option, particularly on buses and Tubes so unless you live in a seriously rural place you will almost definitely end up buying one in the long run. '

Caroline, 33, with Madeleine, six, and Rudy, four

Families become zealous fans of their buggy model, so if you're still doubtful about it doing the right job, suffering from buggy envy or it just doesn't seem to work for you then consider passing it on and getting another that better suits your needs. However wasteful this might seem, a good buggy is always a great car substitute.

'My husband, Mark, wasn't into baby stuff, but he likes gadgets and came across a Canadian buggy called Chariot. It's basically a bike trailer that you can use as a buggy as well. You can use it with a fixed front wheel, or supermarket wheels or a hiking harness, or attach skis to it! And you can attach to the back of the bike as well. It's really simple to clip on or clip off. Since Oliver has been four or five months I've been able to cycle into town, unhook the bike and then slot on buggy wheels. It gets lots of attention. '

Jude, 34, with Oliver, one

Buggy lingo buster

ATP (all-terrain pram) – If James Bond had kids then he'd be using the buggyworld's 4x4 – it's a lightweight three-wheeler than can be wheeled on sandy beaches and along footpaths (plus some have a double-decker fitting so you could use with baby number two). But only go for this if you can cope with the size. Where will you keep it at home? Will it fit on a bus? Can you fold it up to fit in the back of a car or taxi boot? Even if it passes these tests you may find that it won't fit into the buggy park at your child's daycare provider, which may mean you will need two buggies. Keeping in good condition: use a bike pump to keep the tyres at the right pressure.

Designer buggies – a model like the popular Bugaboo is expensive (especially once you include the accessories), but also easy to steer and park and has holders for drinks and shopping space.

Posh prams – the pram base could double as a Moses basket/carry cot so your little prince and princess can be wheeled around in the state they will soon become accustomed to.

Basic easy fold-up buggy (aka umbrella-style buggy) – versatile and affordable. Also good if you need to park a buggy in a tiny space at home or while your baby is at daycare.

Accessories – you will make use of a **sunshade** and a **rain cover** but these don't have to be matching, and you could improvise. Muslins (secured with pegs, parcel tape or clip-on toys) are adaptable sunshades. Rain covers are essential, even if your buggy has a hood, but they are not well made and unless you're careful you could go through two or three during your baby's buggy's career. You are sure to need to use your buggy for carrying things around (not just snacks and your nappy-changing bag) so try and make sure it has an **under-carriage tray**, or is well enough balanced that it doesn't tip over too scarily when you overload the handles with heavy shopping bags. If you don't want to always use a double-decker or a double buggy (which can be a problem getting through narrow doorways) and have at least one child old enough to stand then buggy boards are brilliant. Children find them fun and they also offer a tired child a rest.

Buggy repair

Too many of us accept the idea that a faulty item costs more to mend than replace so if you have a Maclaren buggy – a spin-off by the F1 racing car team created by grandad Maclaren when his daughter had a baby – you are in luck as these come with a basic year's warranty (the 2008 models onwards have a lifetime warranty) as well as a network of service centres for repairs. Find out where your nearest is at www.maclaren-baby.com. This warranty doesn't cover fading covers, use with other children, second-hand purchases or the normal wearing down of wheels, but it is still an incentive to keep the receipt. To keep your buggy in good order look out for:

○ Torn foam handles (babies and dogs chew these, and stressed mums claw them) can be mended with gaffer tape.
○ Loose rivets are fixable with a simple nut and screw.
○ If you've got an ATP you may need to pump up the tyres regularly. If you don't already know, learn how to fix a puncture before the air hisses out.
○ Worn front and back tyres are for the skilled handyman or just head for a repair shop.
○ Torn waterproof covers can be patched with gaffer tape. They get brittle so store carefully, ideally out of direct sun.

The more of us who get our broken buggy fixed up and then share the phone number of the repair centre with a friend or two, the better for all of us. It helps to keep skilled buggy mechanics in work, backs a local business and keeps another buggy out of landfill.

Tip

Organise your own Dr Buggy session where mums get together to tighten rivets, pump tyres and swap info about buggy repairs.

Buggy fun and fitness

Pushy mums may sound like a joke, but wheeling your child around in a buggy is a great way to shed your pregnancy weight without really noticing; pushing a buggy uses up 86 calories an hour. Now add the shopping, a toddler on a buggy board, a double decker with a baby sleeping on the bottom and make a couple of trips a day and, bingo, you are doing Olympic-level training. Once you've passed your six-week check (or eight–ten-week check if you've had a caesarean) then you can try

Travelling to school

Children go to school when they are rising five – unless you are home educating (see www.education-otherwise.org). Like many families with young children, we had one child in big school (primary) and a toddler at nursery located in the opposite direction, plus a job to get to. Start time for all three was 9 a.m. That's when the juggling really starts: we'd speed walk a buggy to the nursery, or take a child on the back seat of a bike, or run to the right place. We were invariably late for two of our appointments, sometimes all three. The only advantage of this stage of parenting is that you eat up your 10,000 steps a day and stay surprisingly fit. Lots of parents feel obliged to drive their children this way and that around 8.30 a.m. and 3 p.m., often combining it with shopping trips, work or a chance to meet with friends. Without children, it is tempting to blame the school-run traffic for gridlocks, but without institutional change (school and work start times; term times, employers figuring out more family-friendly working arrangements), it is not always fair to blame mum in her car – as long as she's not in a 4x4.

joining a 'mummies and buggies' exercise class, which will guide you through an aerobic workout while your baby stays in their buggy. Some of these classes are indoors, others run in local parks and can be a good way to get to know some more parents in the area (and maybe even overtake them…).

> I really enjoy going to "buggy fit". It's a post-natal class – but a lot of mums stay for as long as the babies stay in their buggy. It's very sociable as well and we always go for a cup of tea afterwards. Sometimes if we stop to work on our tummies on our mats on the beach it gives a chance for the babies to have a play too. But running along with the buggies the motion sends the babies off to sleep.
>
> Jude, 34, with Oliver, one

Passing on your buggy

Considering how expensive buggies have become, it is astonishing how many people dump unwanted prams and pushchairs. Over the past five years I've rescued around ten abandoned but 100% working buggies from skips and country footpaths, then brushed off any dirt and donated them to a charity shop or offered them on Freecycle. Some dumped buggies have very minor problems – their tyres need pumping up, a screw has fallen off or they squeak.

Obvious places to pass on your buggy: advertise at a place new mums go, offer on Freecycle, sell on eBay. Also try community noticeboards at your library, newsagent or nearest nurseries. Places of worship can often find homes for your unwanted baby kit, especially those working with the poorest people or linked to refugee centres.

Buggy second life

> We got a proper woodworker to make us a go-kart. He
> had an idea of how to do it and had the proper tools, so
> I would say to find a handy man type and pay him/her
> to help you do it. We couldn't have done it without
> help or having proper tools.
Rachel, 44, with George, 11, Tobias, nine, and Arthur, six

Old pram chassis used to be routinely turned into go-karts. If
you like trying out unusual containers to grow plants you
could park up your unwanted pram, box in the seat with
strong plastic and turn it into a mini mobile herb garden.

Public Transport

> We have no car but I find getting around London on
> public transport very manageable. I used a German-
> made sling exclusively for the first year of his life but
> am now also using a pram on buses, but still a carrier
> when we have to take the Tube. He loves being up high
> on my back looking around over my shoulder and
> making lots of contact with strangers on the way.
Tina, 32, with Atreyu, 19 months

Just as the old Daleks (pre Russell T Davis's tweaks) couldn't
get up stairs, for people with babies it's steps that make public
transport difficult. Although some of the newer buses can fit
as many as four buggies, you still have to be able to tilt them
up a steep step and negotiate an exit. The good thing is that

lots of people on the bus will know what it's like which is probably why, even at crowded times, and if you're willing to ask, you are sure to be surprised how helpful so many people will be.

It's the same story on undergrounds and trains, where dealing with stairs at some point is inevitable. Don't expect staff to help, but you are likely to find other transport users willing to lift your buggy, especially if you've made it lighter by taking the baby out just for the steps. However, the experience is far better if you try and avoid rush hour.

> It's worth knowing that most trains have carriages for disabled people, and if you get on there, there's usually lots of space for buggies – just be aware that the space may have to be given up if needed by a wheelchair user. On most trains, this carriage is actually marked from the outside. For example, on the trains from Waterloo to Dover, there's a big blue flash above the doors.
> Sally, 38, with Anna, two

When running well, travelling by train is an experience that beats any other method of transport – and it's a brilliant way to see more of the UK and Europe. In a train you just sit at your seat, feed your child and know that you will arrive the time you said you would. The drawbacks for train travel are small: you need to be organised enough to buy your ticket before the day of your journey to get a decent discount, be able to stick to these times and have enough snacks and entertainment to keep crawlers and toddlers busy at their seat. It helps if you ask for seats in the family carriage.

' We didn't want to fly to France so we took Robin on holiday on a train when she was five months old. It was lovely: Eurostar is brilliant, French trains are great, big and spacious, and loads of people talked to her. It was a lot of fun. Even in Paris on the Metro people helped us with buggy and rucksacks. It made the trip more social. '

Jo, 37, with Robin, 15 months

If your child is a crawler or older and getting restless on a long train journey a good way of getting some emergency calmness out of them is to have packed a sugar-free lollipop. Or just get off your seat and, with your toddler, walk up and down the aisle or make a journey towards the toilets or go choose a snack from the buffet car.

I met Caroline, a 33-year-old mum of two, when we both had an unexpected hour and half bus ride for part of what should have been a long train journey from Wales to London. To occupy her toddlers on long journeys, she tries to:

- ○ Book a seat (ask if there's a children's carriage so you don't get put in the designated silent carriage)
- ○ Breastfeed
- ○ Show films on a laptop
- ○ Tell stories
- ○ Sing nursery rhymes, particularly the ones that go on forever such as 'Ten Green Bottles'
- ○ Take books
- ○ Remember markers and paper
- ○ Provide lots of sugar-free, not too messy food, e.g., bread, fruit, ricecakes, apple crisps, dried fruit, vegetable sticks, humous for dipping, fruit pots

○ **For travel sickness:** try the Neal's Yard roll-on aroma-
therapy smell or wrist bands, or homeopathic kits can be
bought from helios.co.uk

Cycling

For anyone interested in staying fit, or just liking being
outside, bikes are brilliant. Compared to a car, bikes run on
ricecake crumbs. But cycle experts suggest you should spend
a large chunk of your bike budget on a really secure lock
(and maybe insurance too). In urban areas you will need two
locks – a steel, tight-fitting D-lock that ideally you attach to
a solid metal post and then though your back wheel and
frame. In a city you should also add a semi-flexible cable
lock (although they are easy enough to cut with the right
tools) which can be looped through your front and back
wheels to deter any opportunistic thieving, or at least delay
a thief's attempts.

As with buggies you may find that you need several types
of bike or bike seat to suit your child's/children's needs.

'I cycle a lot with both my children on the bike, and as
well as several rear bike seats, I have two types of front
bike seat. One is called a "wee-ride", which is one
where you screw the seat on a metal bar between
the saddle-post and the handlebars. I also have a
Dutch seat that goes on the handlebars.'
Marian, 37, with Leah, three, and Nathan, one

Even if your nearly three-year-old is adept at using a pedal-free bike or learns how to do without stabilisers few roads are suitable for pre-schoolers to use. However, experience on a tag-along bike or even a bike seat behind you probably helps introduce roadcraft. Children can help listen out for traffic, tell you to pull over when they hear a siren or point out bike parking spots and, best of all, you maintain – or improve – your fitness.

If you are used to cycling, adding a child to a purpose-made child seat is not difficult, although you may find your journey is a bit slower. If you are not used to cycling remember never to overtake an HGV that might turn left, and be sure at junctions shared with a lorry that the driver can actually see you. Cyclists are easier to see if they (and their passengers) don high-vis jackets, fix fluorescent strips on their bikes and choose brightly coloured back panniers. Make sure you have working cycle lights; some people use these during the day for extra visibility. To gain confidence cycling, here are some tips:

- Find a bike buddy to practise your route. This person will show you the fastest, or most traffic-free, route for any journey you'd like to make by bike regularly. Find them by contacting the cycle officer (or sustainability unit) at your council.
- Try taking a holiday at Centre Parcs (or similar) which has traffic-free routes throughout its holiday camps and can be a great place to hire different types of bikes and get your rusty cycle riding skills honed.
- Try hiring a bike so you can use an off-road stretch. There's a huge choice of routes – see www.sustrans.org.uk.

Cycling in comfort with kids

CASE STUDY

Oliver Taylor from London Recumbents (www.londonre-cumbents.com) – a company that rents bikes at Battersea Park and sells the sort of range of bikes for family use that make you think you are in Holland or Germany – has some good ideas about how to cycle with kids. 'You can put a baby on a bike as soon as the baby can hold its head up without support. With rear child carriers, the kid will sleep leaning against your back. Helmets for you and the baby are advised, as much for reassuring other people as for your own safety.'

'Don't fuss about what to get, just get a bike and a child seat. But if you are looking for the bike to grow with your family try a tandem. Make sure that whatever model you buy is strong enough and built appropriately for the task in hand. Don't get the cheapest thing you can find. Some countries have a better reputation than others for produc-tion values. Also, don't think about how expensive the bike is, think about the value that it will give you in years to come – and not just the financial savings of not using a car, there's social value too and, most important of all here, the positive experiences you will be giving your children.'

The downside to using the bucket bike or rickshaw to take my three children to nursery/school is that, like kids in cars, they still get a lift to school so they miss out on having to learn the reality of traffic or crossing roads. But it's much more fun in the mornings and everyone enjoys it, and they all love getting their friends to have a lift. As I cycle along they get waved at and admired. The novelty means the children are the centre of attention on the way to school. We also use it for shopping, carting plants, guitars, stuff for the recycling centre – any transport job, really.

"

Adam, 46, with Martha, 11, Megan, nine, and Francis, five

Here's a guide to getting children out and about on bikes:

○ **Under-one-year-olds and bikes** – wait until their head and neck are strong (perhaps nine months), then get them a helmet and you are ready to roll. Try a front or back child's bike seat.

○ **One child and you on a bike** – use a front or back bike seat.

○ **Two children and you on a bike** – lots of choice. You could fit both a front and back bike seat when they are small. Or you could use a tandem and a front bike seat if you have a one-year-old and a rising four year old. Or use a bike bucket (trike). Even on a trike it's a good precaution to get your child wearing a helmet. If she resists let her decorate it with stickers.

○ **Three children, you and a bike** – try a bike bucket (trike) with a baby seat fitted to the back. Or get a rickshaw.

○ **When your child can pedal themselves** – tow-along tandems are great for giving road skills and confidence. Older two-year-olds also love the pedal-free bikes as a way of travelling long distances on pavements. You may find this improves their balance so much that learning to ride a real bike is easier, but every child will take a different amount of time.

- **No space but you want a bike for an occasional trip** – get a folding bike.
- **When's my child old enough to cycle on the road alone?** – this is your call, but the first RoSPA cycle proficiency test cannot be taken until your child is over the age of nine.
- **What's taboo** – it is illegal for children to cycle on the pavements, but a lot safer. If you do use pavements make your children pedal slowly, be extremely polite and teach them to stop and pull over when someone elderly is approaching.

Driving

> We found you could buy a second-hand Prius £3000–4,000 cheaper than new [before the Toyota accelerator scare]. Then we looked at the costs of running it and saw that a Prius is much lower than the average car for tax, parking permit and petrol. It's either petrol- or electric-powered and it automatically chooses which power to use. Whenever you brake you power up the battery, so if it's been powered up you can drive on electricity. The downside is that it's silent. I've found that people cross the road with their ears so you have to be very careful driving.
>
> Andrea, 35, four months pregnant, with Zak, one

Our society's refusal to give up our love affair with cars is understandable: Cars R Us. And even if you're not so keen, there's a high chance someone else in your family will be, maybe your partner or other relations. Making any change may involve lots of negotiating. Better driving can be very subtle: less braking, less accelerating, combining journeys so your engine's warmed up, keeping your car serviced and your tyres the right pressure, removing the roof rack and keeping windows wound up.

In fact, you don't need a car (or a second car) just because you now have a baby. This is especially true if you are still living in a place that has good public transport, or is not too far from a car hire point, if you have family or friends willing to share a vehicle occasionally, or you live in an area with a car club.

> I think having a baby triggers the "must get a car/pass my driving test" as babies seem to chain you to the home and non-car people want to taste the freedom they used to know, and because of the perception that there's a lot of clobber (and I'll concede there is some). I know a mum who is 42 years old and taking driving lessons just so they can go walking in the great outdoors – ironic? In my opinion the big question if you have a car while they're wee, is how and when do you give it up? One friend gave up their car when their children were about six and eight. Quite tricky and brave to do but she thought her kids would become couch potatoes if they didn't. I expect that's a very rare decision – once you're in a car it's surely hard to get children out again.
>
> Jess, 39, with Connie, six months

According to the RAC website (www.rac.co.uk) it costs between £3,000–£4,000 a year to run a car. That gives any carless family a sizeable imaginary stash to spend on a variety of ways to get around including rail cards, taxis, train fares and car club membership.

People sometimes feel sorry for the families that choose to be carless, because having your own wheels is the estate we're still clinging on to – an illusion of freedom that forgets both environmental consequences, traffic jams and the annual bill. But choosing to be carless – unless you become a hermit – will be good for your fitness as you and the baby make regular trips to the shops, the playground, friends and the doctor's surgery. If you walk or cycle you can always arrive on time too. In contrast, going by car costs money, may take your through a traffic snarl-up (or even put you behind a tractor) and could involve a stressful hunt for a parking spot.

'The children have been on the back of our bikes since they were tiny. Simone has cerebral palsy so now she is at secondary school we have a specially built tandem so she gets some exercise and joins us when we go out as a family. We've recently moved from London to the centre of Woodbridge, Suffolk – most people who felt they could manage without a car in London wouldn't feel that here. Not having a car does restrict us because there are certain activities that we can't do – Lily's friends from school live some distance away so it is not easy to drop Lily off for a brief visit – so those children either come to us and/or the parent comes to collect them. We don't want the hassle of driving, it's unhealthy and environmentally damaging. If we are going a longer distance occasionally we'd hire a car (but it would be primarily for work purposes).'
Sue, 52, with Simone, 12, and Lily, seven

Not having easy access to a car may even improve your family's quality of life, in part because you cannot play taxi driver. This means children get used to going in a buggy, or on a buggy board or walking (skipping, roller blading, cycling, etc.), whatever the weather.

You need a car seat, not a car

' Thinking back, I wish I'd got a buggy that you could clip a car seat to. It would have been useful for getting taxis at the end of a train journey. '
Sally, 38, with Anna, two

Because so many babies are born in hospital (according to 2006 figures, just 18,000 are homebirths), there's a strong chance your baby will take its first drive even before they are a couple of days old. That's why you take a car seat into hospital along with your birthing bag – unless you have an amazing constitution and can walk home with your newborn in a sling, or are close enough to push them home in a buggy.

' Why are people so precious about not having second-hand car seats? I understand there may be a safety aspect if they have been involved in an accident but otherwise, what's the problem, especially for the first car seats which are used for such a short time? I had to have three for Finlay, for my car, his dad's car and his granny's and all were second-hand. '
Laurie, 44, with Maise, 11, and Finlay, two

Taxi firms based near hospitals may provide newborn car seats if you ask when you book. Or if you know you won't be using a car much then you could try and borrow one from someone who knows that car seat's history. The safety advice is not to use a car seat that has been damaged or in a crash. Seats made from expanded polystyrene can be damaged if exposed to temperature extremes, which a summer sun-heated car certainly does.

Sharing journeys and vehicles

A growing number of families now belong to car clubs, which allows them to have a car when they want it. When they don't need the car it is available to everyone else in the club instead of just being parked uselessly outside their home. Car clubs make ambitious claims to reduce pressure on traffic congestion, parking and air quality, according to them one club car can replace five privately owned vehicles. Streetcar, the UK's biggest car club, claims to be tripling in size each year and now has 38,000 members. London has become the car-club mecca but there are clubs in Belfast, Brighton, Cambridge, Edinburgh and Norwich, as well as in rural areas.

Car clubs are membership clubs that have an easy-to-use booking system which gives you 24-hour-a-day, seven-days-a-week access to a car parked somewhere near you. You can book a vehicle for as little a time as half an hour or as long as six months, and you can do so online or via phone or text. The door is opened with a smart card similar to a credit card, you key in your pin number and then put the keys from the glove box into the ignition.

Car clubs take anyone over 18 (minimum ages vary) who has a driving licence and is willing to pay when they want to drive. They may include an annual membership fee. You can use the cars every week, or very occasionally (and you can book your slots months in advance) which makes them a great choice for families who want to use a car at holiday times, perhaps to visit relatives, but don't need one for 49 weeks of the year.

From an environmental point of view joining a car club is a winner. It's good value because you only pay for the time you've booked the car. And it's simple because you don't have to remember your MOT, insurance, servicing, etc. Petrol is usually included in the price, and part of the deal is that when you fill up the tank you pay with a fuel card. This encourages responsible sharing – why wouldn't you leave a full tank for the next driver? Best of all you always have the most efficient, modern vehicles so you get to try different runarounds and can even rent vans. Using a car club will boost your garage patter no end, which could turn out to be useful if your baby becomes fascinated by vehicles.

Baby steps

Small

- Make an eco kit for the car. Include fold-up buggy with rain cover, plus cloth bags or plastic bags you can reuse at the supermarket.
- Look up bus routes on the web in case you can use them for short trips.
- Share a journey in a taxi or go in a car with a friend.
- Try out a sling (borrow from a friend or have a go holding their baby in a sling when you meet at the park).

○ Find waterproof clothing for everyone in the family. Child-sized umbrellas are less bulky so can fit into handbags and under buggies more easily. Wellies are essential in the UK all year – great for splashing through puddles, dealing with festival mud and taking the chill off bare feet if there's been a heavy summer dew.

Medium

○ Research and buy a Family & Friends railcard, as this will enable you to save pounds on your fare, and book a seat. Babies don't need to be paid for, but having a booked seat for an infant makes longer journeys much more bearable.
○ Share childcare by finding a double buggy to borrow (or buy) so that you can give a friend, or nearby mum or dad, a break spinning two babies around the park.
○ Fix up your bike by booking it in for an annual service, finding a dry place for it to live (or buying it bike pyjamas if it has to live outside). Also up your bike care by regularly pumping up the tyres, oiling the chain and knowing how to mend a puncture.

Large

○ Could you or friends organise a Dr Buggy session or repair workshop in the same way that you can organise a private hairdresser or beautician to come to your house?
○ Join a car club and use it rather than your car. Could you be a car club champion and ask for a car club vehicle to be parked near where you live? You might help get a club into your city/town/village.

○ Think ahead: school runs clog up road routes so find out if the council or a local campaign group needs support to find road transport solutions. Does a bus need rerouting or should there be more buses at a different time? Does a school need cycle parking? Can you volunteer to help escort children on a walking school bus? Is there a way of traffic calming busy roads near you? It could take three or more years to get these changes, so start early enough to make sure your growing baby and their-friends-to-be will benefit in the long run.

Nine
Valuing Local Life

Take your baby with you as you get to know your neighbourhood better. Start by exploring, as you find shops, friends, activities and green spaces but don't be surprised if this knowledge inspires you to make your locale far better for a generation of little 'uns.

> Never doubt that a small group of thoughtful, committed citizens can change the world; indeed, it's the only thing that ever has.
> **Margaret Mead, 1901-1978**

> Having children was what prompted me to take climate change seriously, that and a very well-written *New Scientist* article. It made me realise that it's pointless pulling faces and complaining, and that it's my responsibility to do whatever I can to give my children the best chance of survival in the future. At first I didn't realise how important community is, but it's gradually become obvious that this is the most important survival factor, much more than the factual knowledge, e.g., how to find wild foods and make your own solar heater, although of course these things are important.
> **Jo, 39, with Ben, five, and Sally, two**

Being around your children and their friends has surprising consequences: they make you learn to play and dream again. They make you think about life long term too – even as you answer their immediate needs. At the same time babies give you an intensive workshop in what it's like to live life in the slow lane, they delight in what they are doing, hate to be rushed and then, suddenly, feel so hungry that only you, their mum, can help. Caring for a baby is such a small task, but it is something that links millions of us. It's also the most important job most of us will ever have and yet we learn it as we go along. What I've found striking about bringing up my two girls using green values is that a baby quickly becomes a highly motivating teacher who wants to turn you into an ideal parent. With luck, we learn the skills to be this 'ideal parent' as we are parenting, as much by trial and error as by anticipating our baby as a toddler, teenager or a parent of their own. We imagine the world they will be growing up into and that activates us to do a bit more now in the hope of making that future a better one. It's not the next generation's responsibility to sort out climate change, it's our responsibility right now.

Green values?

Some green values are age-old good parenting skills – a mix of old-fashioned and cooperative. Take the lead by providing:

○ Healthy food
○ Loads of time outdoors, whatever the weather (if you can't chase for one more step try reading a book sitting on the grass, and when your toddler tires of the story get them to

pick grass stalks or look for petals to feed to the characters in the book. Try the *Owl Babies* by Martin Waddell and *Little Miss Muffet Counts to 10* by Emma Chichester)

○ Not too much TV (maybe none). Try DVDs or get busy at community activities, like table-top sales, Christmas markets, chutney party, garden workday, instead

○ Lots of fun – but more DIY than purchasable (e.g., tent in the garden/bedroom rather than big trip to Diggerworld)

○ Pleasure and knowledge of the natural world

○ Appreciation of cultural diversity and respect for all peoples (so you think hard about buying products if they were made at the expense of another family's health/working rights or cause pollution somewhere in the world)

○ Encouragement to find practical solutions to all sorts of problems from an early age, e.g., pulling off socks, getting undressed, getting into/ out of bed safely

Dreaming up changes

' Going around the neighbourhood with my baby made me see the world with different eyes. It makes you notice all the things that could be improved for the sake of the children – and also for all the residents and the environment. I feel that my responsibility towards my kids is to keep a positive vision for the future, and to work towards that. That's why I've been active in the real nappy network and have helped set up a transition town and plastic-bag-free local group. '
Cinzia, 34, with Elfo, five, and Electra, 20 months

As you walk sleepy lanes, dodge passers-by on crowded pavements or run errands allow yourself to dream how the place you live could be even better. Once you start imagining a better neighbourhood it's amazing how fast you can be sucked into thinking which streets would benefit from a 20mph speed limit, or how a toy library could help you meet other new mums and how to link up all those barely used front gardens with keen-to-get on with it veg growers.

In some ways dreaming is a luxury task. You may not be able to dream if you are worrying about paying your rent, unexpected redundancy or coping with a family member's illness. But dreaming is free, can be done at any time and what you dream up for your local community is a great way of getting a new type of conversation going at a baby and toddler group if you really don't feel like talking about sleep training again.

> I managed to help run a weekly baby and toddler group when Toby was about one and a half. It was a great way to meet people and fitted into life easily.
> Gaby, 36, with Barney, nine, and Toby, four

Most public places where babies and children meet (even parks which may have Friends groups) are run by volunteers who are really keen to get help from new people. The best are well organised and will provide a take-over pack to make the handover reasonably painless. For example, One O'Clock clubs have a volunteer organising committee. They may need to raise money to pay for visits, trips or to get things on their wish list (painting aprons, easels, willow bower tunnels, covered sand boxes, raised radish bed, etc.). Anyone is allowed to join these committees (either elected at an annual general meeting or co-opted where there's a skill gap).

> When I first had Finn the temptation was to step down as chair of Saltaire Village Society, but instead I took Finn along to a few meetings when he delighted and annoyed people in turns by sleeping or disrupting proceedings. Not only was I keen to avoid motherhood being perceived as incompatible with being active in the community, but having a child increased my passion and sense of commitment to issues such as the problems of high volumes of traffic. But I did realise that I couldn't commit the time and energy I once had and hence asked sometime to stand as a co-chair which they successfully did – so we essentially now job share the position of chair.
>
> Elaine, 44, with Finn, two, and Niall, two weeks

If you have any time, the skills to project manage or want to be active locally then make it easy for yourself, join a group that is already working towards these sort of aims. Voluntary organisations are also a perfect place to satisfy your desire to create greener set-ups locally – and there's a lot to be learnt at them.

Ideas for fundraising

> I just got £250 worth of trees for Alma's nursery – a children's centre which is very community-orientated – so they can complete their lovely

garden with a living wall between the garden and the park. Yay! I like fundraising when you get results like this!

Penny, 38, with Netta, six, and Alma, three

Here are some ideas for groups with a building and/or grounds that could be used as an income stream to help them raise money for eco improvements or specific activities:

- Rent the play space out for weekend birthday parties for toddlers and their families
- Hold a raffle/auction
- Run a summer or winter fair
- Use for overflow car parking (on market day, for concerts, football matches, village hog roasts, etc.)
- Rent to an after-school or breakfast club
- Rent for community activities (plant sales, cricket games, scout troop, musicians' meet-up/rehearsal, farmers' market, Transition Town meetings)
- Charge for tea, coffee and soft drinks (or put out a donation box)
- Encourage an active local group to donate their raffle funds (say, at an AGM) to your group; get a local business to give the equivalent sum to match the volunteer hours given to your group over a week/month/year

There are lots of ideas about how to fundraise in a child-friendly way at the National Council of Parent Teacher Association's website, www.ncpta.org.uk, although you do need to be part of a member organisation to access this information.

Being active locally

' Whose job is it but ours to try and make our world a
better place? The local council can create a rough and
ready framework – they can take away the recycling,
employ street cleaners or mow the grass in the park –
but they're just doing it as a job, not because they
really care about my street. I can be effective because I
really care. And luckily I don't have to do it by myself. '
Jo, 39, with Ben, five, and Sally, two

It's families – whatever their make-up – that raise children.
This allows little ones to absorb, as if by osmosis, life skills such
as home cooking, gardening, cleaning, breastfeeding, pet care,
repair jobs, etc. (as well as turning on the TV, where to hunt
for lost trainers/keys/purse, putting out the recycling, etc.).
But as the well-known Nigerian proverb spells out, mum or
dad can't do it all themselves because 'It takes a village to raise
a child'.

Though few of us have an extended family living nearby,
we can create a similar effect by becoming better acquainted
with the people who live in our neighbourhood. They may
shop at similar stores, visit the same doctor or place of worship,
or simply know when the recycling is collected. That shared
experience can be very powerful when it comes to making
changes in your neighbourhood. It's a glue that helps us trust
each other and can inspire us to keep on doing, chatting,
pestering and organising, because we know it's making the
place so much better for us (and all the kids).

The village experience   CASE STUDY

To give your baby the benefit of a village experience, you can try to emulate the way real villagers still integrate their children into every part of their lives. Anna Craven, 68, trained as an anthropologist and spent 20 years living in remote parts of Africa and the Pacific Islands. Her two children, now 31 and 28, were born in the Solomon Islands in the South Pacific, but when Anna's marriage broke up she moved back to Yorkshire and there worked out how to recreate the best bits of community life.

'You pass on life skills subliminally – by creating family habits rather than instructing children what to do as if they were in a classroom. If you think of Inuit or Ghanian village communities the children learn by example. They watch, they imitate, they're not told. When they start experimenting they develop their own skills. Adults do things with their children – making pots, farming, looking after younger siblings – things that are appropriate to their age and capability. They let even small children handle large bush knives. They don't expect a lot from a child before it 'knows sense' at around the age of four, or 'can reason well' at around eight or ten. Because we don't live close to our extended families, or have a safe community space under the village mango tree, we have lost these skills of socialisation.

'You can bring this experience back. You can let them do things and learn to observe. For instance, you could give your children a little patch of garden to grow their own lettuce. It's so exciting – even if the slugs eat a lot of the crop. Or take children to see lambs being born and let them observe what happens to the placenta – sheepdogs eat it. Tell them that sheep can recognise up to 50 faces, then see if they can pick out different ewes in the flock. Early on you can show them how to use phones and tape recorders properly rather than telling them not to touch. Or go for walks in the woods and identify plants and flowers, and trees by silhouette, by their seeds, flowers or leaves. As children get a little bit older give them adult handbooks – for dog breeds, shells, trees, sea creatures, birds and even posters for sheep – which are packed with information: make it a kind of detective game. Involve them in anything to do with practical life, so that they grow up wanting to learn for themselves.'

If you want something done then you can either have a go yourself, or, better still, tap into the networks that already exist which might have the power to make great changes. This probably won't mean talking to your MP, it's more likely to be finding out who your local councillor is, or which councillor heads the environmental portfolio. It could mean joining a political party – but probably not, because most politically active groups tend to hold evening meetings which are difficult times to make for families with under-threes, even if babysitting costs are provided. It might also mean going to the library or on to the net and discovering active local groups who are sure to need help, or may even be looking for an issue to focus on.

Ready, steady, inspiration

1. Be inspired on holiday

In France it is normal to have great al fresco food markets and summer Sundays when the main town streets are closed to traffic. In the UK some towns and cities hold one car-free day in September or close roads for an annual event, like a street party or community fete. If holiday tales involve nightmare flights or tend to break your carbon budget you might find yourself thinking more about how to get around.

For 20 years my friends and I never talked about politics: we wanted to stay friends! But after seeing the short YouTube film by Rebecca Frayn, *When I Grow Up* (which shows primary school children near Heathrow talking about "When I grow up" – except you can't hear what they say because planes overhead drown out their words) we discussed what we'd say to our children about letting Heathrow airport have another runway. As a consumer there's pressure to do something greener – like insulate or use energy-efficient light bulbs, but I'm not stupid, I know this isn't going to make a blind bit of difference. But there are people in government whose job could make a difference. I think of myself as an activist-lite, I've never scaled a building or been arrested. I look as if I read the *Daily Mail*, but we are getting our message across. It works because we aren't perfect. We're able to say, "You know what, I took a plane flight but I still want change." What's happening to the climate will effect every single person, so we say when there's an action "just show up". '

Jennifer Nadel, ITN journalist, mum of two and co-founder of WeCAN stop climate change, www.wecan.uk.com

2. Be inspired on a work trip

In Holland (and Germany) it is normal to cycle – not just because it is flat – but because many urban areas are designed to give cars and pedestrians equal rights. If vehicles are moving slower then the streets get safer. Already many places in the UK are working to make residential streets 20mph zones. As you walk around a 20mph zone you'll find that it is a much friend-lier place – car drivers will catch your eye and may wave you across the road. And you may wave or smile to thank them.

' Seeing entire families on a bike in Indonesia made a difference to me. If they could get five on, then surely I could get two children on a bike with me? I also remember visiting my brother in Germany and seeing people cycling quite happily with kids on a bike, but there they have proper cycle lanes separated from traffic. '

Kirsty, 44, with Hamish, eight, and George, six

3. Be empowered by new laws

Thanks to the Sustainable Communities Act, which was passed in October 2007, there are now more formal ways of green-ing the neighbourhood. This law can help save local post offices, local shops, independently owned pubs, brings local community representatives on to council panels – with a stress on under-represented groups (young people, older people, ethnic minorities, etc.). There are some useful info sheets about how this act works and how to make full use of it at www.localworks.org and www.unlockdemocracy.org.uk.

4. Be ready to help your nearest school

> I'm a parent governor of the school. I wanted to be involved locally. It's where you live, where you are, where your children are growing up, it's the people they are meeting, places they are playing.
> Anna, 36, with Freddie, four, and Elsie, two

There are close to 350,000 governor places in England, making governors the largest volunteer force in the country. You do not have to have a child at the school, you could volunteer to be a governor even if you're in the planning stages of having a baby. Most governorships are for three years but there is often an opportunity to be co-opted without the need for an election. Find out more at www.direct.gov.uk.en/parents or visit www.sgoss.org.uk.

5. Copy a really good idea

Already there are hundreds of towns copycating eco-initiatives such as the plastic-bag-free movement, begun in Modbury, Devon in 2007 and now embraced by more than 100 towns. The slow food movement is a little older, begun in 1989 as an antidote to fast food and fast life. It began in Bra, Italy but in the UK has a stronghold in the south-west, and Bristol is the unofficial capital. Are there other local people wanting to unleash a transition town plan in your area? The first transition town in the UK was Totnes, but since then Lewes, Brighton

& Hove, Forres, Lewes, Maidenhead, Omar, Tring and York are all working to respond to the twin challenges of dealing with peak oil and tackling climate change, find out more at www.transitiontowns.org. Even the government is trying to create at least four new eco towns – so called because they will be drive-free zones with parking at the town edges, allotments and recycling facilities – although resistance from neighbours is high because they are likely to be built in rural areas.

Easy ideas to copy include growing food in the front garden, tool shares/swaps, pot luck feasts, clothes exchange, bookclubs, CRAGS – carbon rationing action groups – campaigning groups, veg co-ops and shared food deliveries. Bigger ideas ripe for copying include:

- Community green spaces and gardens (e.g., Todmorden in Yorkshire is turning itself into one big allotment)
- Off-road footpaths and cycle tracks
- Farmers' markets, see www.farmersmarkets.net
- Festivals (art, gastro, music, etc.)

‘ I run two stalls at farmers' markets to promote organic and fair-trade products, but mostly to expand our Re-fill Station (where people refill their empty plastic bottles with Ecover, Faith in nature and Bio products). The markets are at East Oxford Primary School and another located in Wolvercote Primary School, Oxfordshire. These markets are great because people from all walks of life can come and buy ethical stuff and share more than a coffee and home-made cake, share common views on sustainability and how to make a humble but effective impact in our near

environment. So that's how our children (i.e., the children of sellers and customers) are part of a little, local world in which values speak for themselves. *'*
Rina, 40, with daughters aged ten and eight

6. Celebrate the good things at a neighbourhood party

A summer fete, winter festival or street party is often a local highlight. It may be that where you live there's already an event pencilled in, but it could be so much better – or it could be in need of baby-friendly suggestions from a local like you. Even if you still feel overwhelmed by parenthood you lose nothing by making sure you attend a community event. At the very least you may meet people with children the same age as yours who will wave at you whenever they next see you in the area – at the best you might even make new friends.

' Helping organise our street party was also a very do-able community activity with young children, but best to do it as part of a group – www.streetsalive.net tells you all you'll ever need to know about street parties. *'*
Gaby, 36, with Barney, nine, and Toby, four

Get skilled up

Working towards a low-carbon neighbourhood may make you realise how many skills need honing – the big problem is how to learn when you've got to look after your little one too. However child friendly a course seems – orchard backdrop, big garden, cosy rooms – it is best to ask if you and your baby, or young child, will be welcome. At LILI, the low-impact living initiative in Buckinghamshire (in Machynlleth, Wales there's CAT – the Centre for Alternative Technology) you can find a range of courses that will develop practical skills from making biodiesel to keeping chickens. But as course administrator, Taryn, points out: 'You can't focus on a course if you are looking after a baby or a toddler and we'd never want children on a building course. But it depends, and we do get people asking if they can bring a child with them every four months or so. At the Low-Impact Living Initiative we ran one DIY for beginners course and two single mums brought their friend to look after their three children while they did the course. We've also had a tutor who was breastfeeding but her partner was able to look after the baby the rest of the time so she could do the training without being distracted.'

Babies are fabulously portable, they will not insist on attending music, swimming and singing classes during your maternity leave or childcare days. What they want is to be with you. It's not always easy in a baby-unfriendly culture to manage this so consider the options and aim for the baby-friendly choice. That doesn't mean ghettoising yourself for all those pre-school years in places only children go, it's just a suggestion that babies and children are an inspiring part of our lives so keep that enthusiasm by opting to be part of the events and activities that give that feeling back to you too.

Baby steps

Small

○ Try out a One O'Clock club (or other local meeting point for families with 0–5-year-olds).

○ Go to a community event, perhaps meet up with friends there? If it's not for you you can always leave early. Worst-case scenario: you're forced to buy a delicious cake.

Medium

○ Team up with another family and try sharing childcare, maybe for just an hour or two a week. Does it give you time to help set up or help out a community event?

○ Improve a rusty skill or learn something new (you don't have to go on a formal course, you can practise at home).

○ Love a communal bit of land (e.g., water, weed, plant up wasted areas, tree pits, hanging baskets, etc.).

Large

○ Find out if your neighbours would like to have a small street party or summer fair and get the planning going by organising the first meeting.

○ Be heard: offer solutions not just complaints. Be ready to volunteer and do stuff to improve your neighbourhood. During the daytime, it's easy for you and a baby to give out posters, surveys or spread the word about what's going on. At nighttime, or when your baby is asleep, you can telephone around, email or spread the word on the Internet.

Conclusion
Next Steps

Having a baby focuses the mind sharply on the future. Our children have so much potential that it can only benefit society if there were more family-friendly work–life choices available. Living green is not a theory, it's a practical, hands-on response to climate change and provides a system for raising happy, healthy and creative children. In this chapter meet families who choose to live thriftily and creatively and with an eye on choosing an eco-friendly way of life. See for yourself the benefits of an eco-drenched childhood.

'Green parenting helps you have children very cheaply, and that's really important in times of recession and to help parents have a work–life balance. My partner and I have found it's completely doable to drop our hours. This is good environmentally, and we are there for our kids.'

Anna, 36, with Freddie, four and Elsie, two

Life can be so hectic that it's easy to find your efforts to raise a cute eco-bunny baby misfire. There are also moments when you may doubt whether your small efforts can translate into the sort of beneficial impact needed to tackle climate change and wasteful over-consumption. This is the point when you need to remember we're all just doing our best, no one is wilfully trying to raise their baby to wreck the planet. Why would they?

Unfortunately, wrecking the planet remains a side effect of conventional childrearing and our hectic work–life balance, particularly in the developed world. If you feel your efforts to green your life are mostly on hold due to work or other circumstances, a positive way to support the people who are on the green frontline is to show interest in what they want to achieve or even back them.

Rethinking jobs

'We both work part time – I realise this is a luxury but we've not done nursery or other childcare before the age of three and juggle our work hours between us. We don't have much money but have a very high quality of life – I hope this will be more important than money to our children when they are older. '

Zoe, 39, with Mati, six, and Pip, three

Private daycare eats up salaries, yet it is what most of us without obliging family members feel that we have to do. Childcare isn't all bad: it gives you the time to get back to the office after child-birth and that might give you the confidence (and cash) to figure out a better way of using your professional skills. But it is more likely to enable you to be tumbled into a frenetic work style that will eventually compromise your own well-being as you agonise about how to afford to make essential changes.

Jonathan Rutherford, a dad, professor of Cultural Studies at Middlesex University and editor of Soundings Journal (www.soundings.co.uk), thinks that although we can help our children make green first steps, parents need the government to make some rather bigger strides dealing with equity and who minds the baby. As he puts it:

> There can be no satisfactory answers to how to be good mothers and fathers without restructuring the economy to take account of the family needs of small children and babies. Until we make these structural changes in the labour market; in corporate policy towards employment, fatherhood and motherhood, equal pay for men and women and a comprehensive system of not-for-profit childcare, we'll have a voluntarism which means only a small number will be able to choose alternative models of parenting. We need government to build a care economy that includes properly funded nurseries staffed by well-paid graduates, trained in social pedegogy and child development. No cheap options, no crap for children living in poverty. Green parenting means equality and good quality for all, so that parents can foster the love and care children need to grow and flourish. Parents need to make our own individual choices about what is best for each of us and that means a radically new kind of public provision not a private market in childcare. Green parenting won't be a planet saver as a lifestyle option, it has to be a big public political issue.

The mystery is why more people don't challenge the status quo, or why being a stay-at-home mum – even for a short time – is not rewarded with much respect. What people do or earn is still considered more important than how we raise our children. The result is that lots of women rush back to work and attempt to juggle office tasks with child and household management in a giant game of compromise.

> Thinking about the *Continuum Concept* (keeping your baby close to you, breastfeeding, co-sleeping, using a sling) – one of the main things about this lifestyle choice is that one of the parents (probably the mother...) would probably need to give up work (although the book says just bring the baby to work, I can't imagine many jobs actually letting you, or it being practical to do so). Working is another factor with using greener nappies or not as I've found nurseries/nannies/ childminders in general prefer not to use terries.
>
> Sarra, 36, with Saskia, four, Alfie, two, and Ivan, three

I spent at least four years rushing from nanny or nursery to job and back again. The childcare ate nearly 100% of my wage (admittedly part-time). No surprise that I felt permanently on the edge of emotional and financial disaster, despite having lucked out by finding a three-day-a-week job (when my eldest daughter was one year old) that closely matched my skills, and which I could cycle to. If this was having it all, it did not feel worth it.

The challenge is could we all work in different ways, maybe short weeks, or job-sharing? Could we work hard for a company but not have to give our soul with family-unfriendly long hours, after-hour care and weekend work? Could we have time to think about living more simply, with time to clean our homes and play with our kids rather than employ other women to do this? Could professionals be encouraged to work less hours so that they can also do things they love or even to learn some life-changing skills? Could we all free ourselves from the 35-hour-week tyranny and make time to reuse and repair stuff, rather than live with such limited me-time that we've no time to find what we need, unless it is new?

This new way of working would share out the salaries and gives all workers (especially dads) more time for their family or their own creative projects. To fast track eco-friendly childcare into family and work life is tricky on your own and depends on family finances/relationships. Wherever your life is now, know that you can do some things, and the other changes need institutional backing and political will. Until then take inspiration from your growing child who will know you are always a super hero. What better role model could there be for any child?

Work-life balance

○ Have you got a vision of how you would like to be working – does it leave you enough room to raise money, enjoy your child and be creative? Is it the way you are working now?

○ Can you work out a plan that will allow you to achieve those work–life changes?

○ Are you a good example to your child, or are your children now the main project?

○ Can you downshift or find a way to make your household expenses low enough to allow you to work nearer to home, or even at home?

○ Is your life work-friendly or child-friendly? Which way do you want it to be?

○ Upgrade your own pester power: stand as an MP… or go to one of your MPs surgeries and talk to them about what they could do to make the future better for the next generation.

What Will My Kids Think?

If you've read this far, then you'll know parents need to pick out the best bits of eco-living to suit their own lifestyles. And they all do it differently, which means there's no obligation to give up TV, turn off the heating or knit your rabbit's loose hair into tank tops – although you may do all those things. Some of us wash nappies and bake our own bread, but there's no rule that says soaking and kneading are obligatory. What's important is that as we raise our children we prepare them to cope with a very different world. By sharing your own love of nature – or growing it as your babies grow – and introducing children to low carbon ways of living at home and in the neighbourhood, we are also helping a new generation learn respect for others (whether human or animal). It's a humane way of living and could start off a life to be proud of. The next section asks school-aged children and adults brought up in a green way how they rated the green experience. Is it worth bringing up baby in an eco-friendly way? Over to them:

What's so great about being brought up in a green way?

School kids

> You don't have to die in aeroplane crashes because we never go on them. You don't have to pay money for food when you have homegrown fruit and vegetables. If you buy [English] toys and food in season that means you don't have to have it sent over in ships or planes, which I think stops the climate getting so bad.

My friends like playing in my garden on the swing but sometimes they get scared by the hens.

Nell, seven

Looking after children in a green way is just like having a hamster. You feed them and don't forget them.

Elsa, eight

All my friends love animals, so I talk to them about that to help them understand climate change.

Ciara, nine

Being brought up green is really good. I kind of feel different to my friends because I know about vegetables, plants, trees and the climate, but they know about trainers, jeans, clothes and phones. But we can still be friends! My mum and dad don't have much money, but I like them being around so much as I know some of my friends really miss seeing their parents even if they have really posh holidays. I want to be an apothecary – I like making sleep potions. You can go to Neal's Yard or pick mint and lavender and stuff like that from your front garden.

Lola, 11

It's good to bring up children in a green way. If no one cared about the environment we'd all die [goes into complex story about CO_2, carbon capture and trees – impressive detail for an adult, even]. My parents encouraged me to recycle and compost so when me and my friends eat our lunch in the back field of school I tell them not to litter. I try to look after the environment because I love it. [Being brought up green] feels the same as anyone else, except my friends like going to Burger King. I don't really like that because I think fast-food chains might be cruel to animals. I love going to the Eden Project in Cornwall. When I was last there we had a big picnic with strawberries from Cornwall and they were so good. At school I'm an eco rep and we have our own veg patch. Today we picked our own strawberries and gooseberries and they were so good. We knew what had gone into them, no yucky stuff. I really like animals – I put bird food out and for Christmas my auntie sponsored this donkey for a year for me. He's called Akiki. My friend is funny, if she has an apple core or anything she asks if it is biodegradable, and I'll say yes. Then she knows where to put it. Me and my mum turn the computer and TV off at the plug when not using it. We always use energy-efficient light bulbs. I either want to work on crime scene investigations or be a biologist or help animals or do something like my mum or dad do – one helps produce sustainable cities and the other stops illegal logging.

Izzy, 12 (Year 7 at secondary school)

I like living in a green way even if we don't live like other people. I want to keep the world green and not polluted. Even when I grow up I am going to live like this – I can't stop myself now I've been brought up to it. We have an allotment and garden in boxes [raised

beds]. I want to grow vegetables you can roast, like
potatoes and parsnips. I love them. I like to explore
with our bike. My sister thinks I use a lot of effort
cycling – obviously it is a lot of effort, but it's good.
We went for a really long cycle in Woodbridge and I
really enjoyed it. I've gone as far as eight miles on a
sponsored cycle ride, I like to help people and I
managed to do it. And there were break places to
have a drink and snacks. At school they recycle paper
but I want to know why they don't recycle cans and
other things. We have an environment officer so I've
mentioned it to her and she's thinking about it.

**Simone, 13 (Year 8 at secondary school), has cerebral palsy.
She uses a laptop in class for writing and has sticks to walk but
always goes to school on a tandem bike.**

Mums looking back at what they did – was it worth it?

We set out to have a "carbon-neutral baby" but didn't
really measure or test this aim. Rosa's just six months
now and so far our goal has led to her doing about 600
miles on my bike, and just 35 miles by car. In accord
with how we live, we've been extremely strict with
ourselves and relatives, only allowing home-made and
second-hand. There have been a few exceptions but not
many. We are currently living off-grid [i.e., with no
mains services such as electricity or gas] in a Spanish
eco project [www.sunseed.org.uk], which we travelled to
by train. I have to be honest and say that since arriving
here it's been difficult to carry on using reusable

nappies but the ones we do use are washed in a bicycle-powered washing machine; when the sun's shining this is a great deal more fun than it sounds. Rosa's a very jolly little soul and, I think, a great advert for green living. I think it's a brilliant way to bring up a child.

Rebecca, 37, with Rosa, six months

I'm not that eco-friendly. When reality hits you with three children under four years, some ideals have to go! I did use re-usable nappies for a time but gave up when Isaac was a few weeks old. I also used Ecover and bought a huge box of it but decided it didn't make the clothes smell nice! However, I do use Freecycle to give away things we don't need and also acquire things we need from there too. The aim is to save perfectly usable things from the tip, hence saving the planet, I suppose. It's a big network and very useful and green.

Lily, with three children

Remembering a super green childhood

I have no doubt that my passion for the environment stems from my mother's love of the countryside. Consciously or not, her infectious enthusiasm for it sowed the seed of my own love for it at a very early age, and led over time to my desire to play my part in protecting it for future generations.

Michael, 27 (recycling officer)

My mum moved out of London to have her own farm in the 1970s. She has polytunnels, makes her own

cheese and bread and lots of jellies and jams. When
I was little we had our own sheep and goats. It was
wonderful when my brothers and I were young, but we
were bored when we were teenagers, as you want to
meet other teenagers. It's quite easy to grow up with
no awareness of where food comes from, but if you
have a goat then you know it makes milk. Obviously,
we can't have a goat in London but I talk to my
children about where milk comes from. Mum still
makes all sorts of juices, jams and jellies. I do it
sometimes if I'm down in Gloucestershire in the right
season, but now I've got very young children I just do
it for fun, not to tide us over.

Sarra, 36, with Saskia, four, Alfie, two, and Ivan, three months

If you make children think or be a certain way they
often rebel in adolescence. In my case my father and
mother [Satish and June Kumar Mitchell, editors of
Resurgence magazine, www.resurgence.org] didn't tell
me how I should think or what the world was like, they
left it for me to work it out for myself. Rather than tell
me what I could or couldn't do they created the
environment they wanted for me. There was no TV, I
played with wooden toys and we had a nice garden so
I was outside most of the time. It's good to bring your
children up in an environment that lets you say yes to
most of their requests – if there is no TV they can't ask
to watch it! Children like to try out a huge range of
things so it is important to have a lot of practical skills
available in the early years. For me (though this was at
a later stage) the Small School, Hartland, Devon

provided a huge range of learning experiences of which at least half were practical and creative and only a few subjects had exams. You never know what skills your child might have – even if they are going to be a lawyer, they may absolutely adore carpentry. It may be a hobby, or something that they do on the side, it may complement their career. We are working in different ways now, there's a move towards part-time jobs or having two very different jobs. For myself I find this is a good balance: keeps your energy levels and productivity high. **'**

Mukti Mitchell, 36, owner of the environmentally friendly Mitchell Yachts (see www.mitchellyachts.co.uk)

When your baby is born something vital happens to your brain. You now know you are responsible for this amazing little person and you will do whatever it takes to do the right thing for that baby. At the same time you suddenly understand – or are even more puzzled by – your own upbringing. You may remember watching nappies dry or having your face wiped. You may be filled with love for your mum, or be furious with someone related to you, or even both, as you realise what they faced dealing with a little you. Unlocking those childhood memories and then distilling them in order to be a decent enough parent is literally a life's work. It's powerful enough to help you make changes; creative enough to dream up new ways of getting what you want. And it gives you courage to be the force of change too.

So here's to your child and all those baby bumps out there – the best change motivators in the world; smiling (from six weeks!) as they direct you to find the best in life for them.

And if we are all lucky that search for the best for your baby will seamlessly lead you on an eco-friendly track towards healthy foods, strong communities, childcare swaps/circles and the creativity to tackle climate change any way possible. Let's hope your journey is enriched even more by laughter, good luck, good health and just the right amount of sleep.

Resources

Useful Websites

Act on CO$_2$ – this is a government-funded website that takes the mystery out of doing your bit. Log on to measure your carbon footprint, offset carbon emissions or even use it to compare the fuel efficiency and carbon dioxide emissions of different types of car. See www.actonco2.direct.gov.uk.

Around Britain without a Plane – this blog follows my family's efforts to see the world without racking up our carbon footprint. Read about our activites at www.around britainnoplane.blogspot.com.

Climate Outreach Information Network (COIN) – provides training, talks and info about living a low-carbon lifestyle. See www.coinet.org.uk.

Energy Saving Trust – a useful government site that helps people make informed decisions about their home's energy-efficiency needs. It is also a good place to look for grant information if you are thinking about adding loft insulation or putting in renewable technologies. See www.energysavingtrust.org.uk.

Forest Stewardship Council – an international independent certification agency that assesses whether wood and wood products (e.g., paper pulp in nappies) have come from well-managed woodlands. See www.fsc-uk.org.

Freecycle – these groups match people who have things they want to get rid of with people who can use them, keeping

usable items out of landfill. Find a local group at
www.uk.freecycle.org.

Friends of the Earth – the UK's most influential environmental campaigning organisation aims to inspire solutions
to environmental problems. See www.foe.co.uk.

Homemade Kids – visit my book's website at www.home
madekids.co.uk for further information and links to more
thrifty, creative and eco-friendly ideas.

NCT (National Childbirth Trust) – the UK's biggest parenting charity. They support parents through pregnancy, birth
and early days of parenthood, offering antenatal and post-
natal courses, local support and reliable information. See
www.nctpregnancyandbabycare.com.

Soil Association – campaigns for organic food and farming. It also runs a certification scheme to ensure that
produce that says it is organic meets set standards. See
www.soilassociation.org.

Sustain – a food and farming alliance that campaigns to
improve food standards. Keep a lookout for The Children's Food Campaign which aims to improve young
people's health and well-being through better food knowledge. See www.sustainweb.org.

Sustrans – see www.sustrans.org.uk for ideas about off-road
and quiet cycle routes. As good for routes to nursery as
holiday planning.

Youth Hostel Association – good value places to stay with
babies/children. Many have been refurbed with energy-
efficient measures and also offer home-cooked, locally
sourced meals. See www.yha.org.uk.

1: Give Your Home a Green Makeover

Calculate your carbon footprint

For the most accurate measurement of your carbon footprint you will need last year's electricity and gas bills. It may help to have a calculator and your old diary (if you have one) to remind you how many miles you travelled using fossil fuel methods. Try one of the many options below to calculate your carbon footprint. You can compare how carbon calculators are ranked at the Climate Outreach & Information Network (COIN) site, www.coinet.org.uk.

- Join hundreds of thousands of people cutting their emissions by 10% each year with friendly guidance from 10:10, see how at www.1010uk.org
- Log on for the carbon calculator at the government-run Act on CO_2, www.actonco2.direct.gov.uk
- You don't even have to log on. Try the questionnaire in *Carbon Calculator* by Mark Lynas (Collins, 2007)
- WWF's footprint calculator at www.footprint.wwf.org.uk
- *Resurgence* magazine has a thorough online carbon dioxide calculator at www.resurgence.org/carboncalculator
- Try the carbon cutter at the Energy Saving Trust, www.energysavingtrust.org.uk
- *An Inconvenient Truth* movie-inspired carbon calculator at www.climatecrisis.net
- If you are interested in measuring your carbon footprint and then reducing it by carbon offsetting (a controversial approach, but it is suitable for home or business) look at www.CO2balance.com

Energy audit help

Borrow this useful book from the library, *How Can I Stop Climate Change* by Friends of the Earth (Collins, 2008). Another great guide is *Carbon Detox* by George Marshall (Gaia Books, 2007). If you want inspiration about simplifying life in a zero-fossil-fuel manner read *Walden*, Henry David Thoreau's classic tale of living the simple life in nineteenth-century America. My husband's book *There's a Hippo in my Cistern*, Pete May (Collins, 2007) is a fun read about living with a green partner.

Meet like-minded people via a Carbon Rationing Action Group. See www.carbonrationing.org.uk.

To keep your energy in by blocking chimneys, try www.chimney-balloon.co.uk.

Mobile phones/masts

For detailed information about what's wrong with mobiles, mobile phone masts and other electro-magnetic devices see www.powerwatch.org.uk. Also see the Stewart Report (Independent Expert Group on Mobile Phones) at www.iegmp. org.uk/report/text.htm, which, back in May 2000, stated that some people's well-being will be effected by the siting of mobile phone base stations near homes, schools etc.

For useful tips (as your children get older) about how to manage mobile phone dependency see www.childalert.co.uk.

Paint

Here is a list of some natural branded paints – have a look at their websites to compare what is on offer and also how to use them.

- Aglaia, www.naturalpaintsonline.co.uk
- Auro, Stroud, www.auro.co.uk, 01452 772020
- Beeck, www.cornishlime.co.uk/html/products.php? category=149
- www.ecomerchant.co.uk
- Ecos, www.ecospaints.com
- Traditional mixes and shades available from Farrow and Ball, www.farrow-ball.com
- Livos, an Australian brand available in the UK. Find info at www.livos.com
- Nutshell, made in the UK, see www.nutshellpaints.co.uk
- Low-Impact Learning Initiative (LILI), www.lowimpact.org, runs courses so you can learn to mix and make your own clay-based paint

Safety

For more info about preventing asthma triggers in your home see www.asthma.org.uk. If you are having trouble managing your child's asthma call the Asthma UK Adviceline on 0800 121 62 44 (9 a.m.–5 p.m. Monday–Friday). Also find out info about managing eczema, and avoiding triggers (especially in the bathroom) see www.eczema.org.

See useful books by Pat Thomas, such as *What's in This Stuff: The essential guide to what's really in the products you buy in the supermarket* (Rodale, 2006).

Timber and timber products

Find out the nearest stockist of timber from a woodland-certified and well-managed supplier, or do a product search at www.fsc-uk.org.

2: Shopping

Certified products

Find out more about the rules and criteria for particular products by looking at the certifying body's rules, or by checking a campaign group's research.

○ Useful insights for organic food/toiletries/textiles, etc. can be found at www.soilassociation.org

○ For Forest Stewardship Council (FSC) certified timber see www.fsc-uk.co.uk

○ For European eco-efficient label requirements see http://ec.europa.eu/environment/gpp/gpp_and_eco_labels_en.htm

○ If you want to know your purchase is vegetarian see www.vegsoc.org, or vegan, see info and links at www.vegansociety.com

Ethical products

Ethical Consumer and Ethical Junction help consumers compare credentials, though both require you to be a member. See www.ethicalconsumer.org and www.ethical-junction.org.

Electrical equipment

Find out where to take broken or unwanted electrical equipment at www.easyweee.com

Fair-trade products

For info about the fair-trade mark (products, requirements, etc.) visit www.fairtrade.org.uk.

Furniture

There are more than 400 depots run by Furniture Reuse Network, www.frn.org.uk, that will collect unwanted furniture and pass on good-quality and reconditioned items to people who really need them.

Shopping and swapping

Sites that offer free and/or good-value items, conversation and ideas, enabling you to find the exact items you need, include:

○ Craigslist at www.craigslist.co.uk
○ eBay online auctions, www.ebay.co.uk
○ Freecycle at www.freecycle.org. Join your local group and benefit from all the items offered close to your home. Also good for getting rid of things you no longer want
○ www.greenbargainsblog.com brings you bargains and tips that don't cost the Earth
○ Gumtree at www.gumtree.com (check out the freebies)
○ www.ooffoo.com, set up by the Natural Collection, encourages a community feel by letting users swap know-how, sell things and share good ideas
○ NCT (National Childbirth Trust) forum, www.nct pregnancyandbabycare.com
○ SwapXchange, www.swapxchange.org (often linked to council websites)

You can also try setting up informal offers/wanted requests on office or neighbourhood email lists.

For an irreverent take on consumer culture, visit the website of Reverend Billy and the Church of Life after Shopping at www.revbilly.com/about-us.

Swish (clothes swap)

See the rules of swishing and a model invite at www.swishing.org.

3: Gifts and celebrations

Cash gifts

Banks can advise you about children's tax-free accounts. Find out about Child Trust Funds at www.childtrustfund.gov.uk.

Celebrations

There are many different ways to celebrate the birth of a child. To find out more about blessingways see www.naturalbirthandbabycare.com. For information on non-religious options see www.humanism.org.uk/ceremonies. For religious options ask at your nearest place of worship.

Fantasy playtime

See the Fairyland Trust for info on family days out at www.fairyland.org.

Mending toys

For ideas about what can be repaired see www.toyrepairs.co.uk (for lost limbs, chipped paint, damaged stuffing, etc.), although it often has a long waiting list. Or to help you start repairing an older toy get inspired by items on show at V&A Museum of Childhood www.vam.ac.uk/moc or Pollock's Toy Museum www.pollockstoymuseum.com.

Nature defecit disorder

There are some interesting ideas about nature deficit disorder at the US's Children and Nature Network at www.childrenandnature.org, which may inspire you and your family to start by making gifts and end up letting the bigger kids patch together their own tent and camp in the garden just for the adventure of it. Also see Richard Louv's *Last Child in the Woods*, (Atlantic Books, 2009) and *Toxic Childhood: How the Modern World is Damaging Our Children and What We Can Do about It* by Sue Palmer (Orion 2006).

As an antidote try looking at *Nature's Playground: Activities, Crafts and Games to Encourage Children to Get Outdoors* by Fiona Danks and Jo Schofield (Frances Lincoln, 2005). Or see the ideas developed by play leaders Edward and Rachel Leigh-Wood, www.playingoutdoors.org.

Party tips

All sorts of companies can help you 'green' your party with recycled paper invites, biodegradable balloons, paper party bags and organic food. Use the web to find local suppliers or borrow their ideas and have a go yourself.

Toy libraries

Not everyone has a toy library close by – you can always suggest a nearby playgroup starts one up, or maybe you could start up something informally with friends. Find your nearest toy library, and also the good toy guide, at the National Association of Toy and Leisure Libraries, www.natll.org.uk.

4: Food – What's Your Child Eating?

Birthing and breastfeeding advice

For extended breastfeeders (anything over a year) the NCT breastfeeding helpline (0300 3300 772, www.nctpregnancyandbabycare.com) and La Leche League (www.laleche.org.uk) can help.

You may find the following books useful:

- ○ *The Politics of Breastfeeding,* Gabrielle Palmer (3rd edition, Pinter and Martin, 2009) makes most readers much more vocal about supporting breastfeeding
- ○ *Nature's Children*, Juliette de Bairacli Levy (Ash Tree, 1996) covers remedies, recipes, folklore and may tempt you into getting goats, is not available in the UK, however you can pick up reprints from Amazon's US site
- ○ *The Food of Love*, Kate Evans (Myriad, 2008) is a great comic strip book on breastfeeding
- ○ For useful combo advice try *Baby-Led Weaning: Helping Your Baby to Love Good Food* by Gill Rapley & Tracy Murkett (Vermilion, 2008)
- ○ Desmond Morris's *Babywatching* (Jonathan Cape, 1999) is a classic book about understanding your baby

Eco-friendly food

Good books on the politics of food:

- *The Killing of the Countryside* (Vintage, 1998) and *We Want Real Food* (Constable, 2008) by Graham Harvey
- *Not on the Label: What Really Goes into the Food on Your Plate* (Penguin, 2004) and *Eat Your Heart Out: Why the Food Business is Bad for the Planet and Your Health* (Penguin, 2008) by Felicity Lawrence
- *Shopped: The Shocking Power of British Supermarkets* (Fourth Estate, 2004) by Joanna Blythman

Good recipe books:

- *Organic Baby & Toddler Cookbook* by Lizzie Vann (Dorling Kindersley, 2008)
- *The Green Kitchen: Techniques and Recipes for Saving Energy and Reducing Waste* by Richard Ehrlich (Kyle Cathie, 2009)

For ideas about how vegans feed their children see www.vegfamily.com/vegan-children/ or the UK site, www.vegansociety.com. Also see *Feeding Your Vegan Infant with Confidence* by Sandra Hood (available from the Vegan Society).

Two fun bedtime reads for young children are Lauren Child's *I Will Not Ever Never Eat a Tomato* (Orchard, 2001) and Katharine Quarmby & Piet Grobler's *Fussy Freya* (Frances Lincoln, London, 2008).

There are some classic storybook recipes that you can't resist making in *Cherry Cake and Ginger Beer* by Jane Brocket (Hodder & Stoughton, 2008). Also see www.yarnstorm.blogs.com.

Fish

Don't eat fish that is endangered, such as cod, unless it comes from Icelandic waters. Farmed fish creates myriad environmental problems so avoid this, too (e.g., trout and salmon). For info about what's an eco-friendly fish choice visit www.msc.org (which has a downloadable pocket-sized guide).

Foraging

Two-year-olds love to find wild food – if you don't take too long. Get in the habit of taking empty bags, secateurs or lidded containers with you for walks so you can take home your finds. It may help to have a good fungi ID book and a copy of Richard Mabey's *Food for Free* (Collins, 2001). Also see Fergus Drennan's website, www.wildmanwildfood.com. He runs courses, prints ideas, explains the law and has some interesting insights into how to make pan-boiled fox, braised squirrel and chickweed all taste delicious.

Gardening and composting

Gardening isn't that easy, but you learn something every time you do it. Good books include Dominic Murphy in *The Playground Potting Shed: A Foolproof Guide to Gardening with Children* (Guardian, 2008).

Improve your food-growing skills by exploring permaculture methods (ideally on a course so you get hands on help). See www.permaculture.org.uk, and find out about seed swapping.

If you have wormery you may know that worms can be tricky to keep alive if you feed too much citrus or let their bin get too cold during winter. Lots of help is available at www.wigglywigglers.co.uk.

For composting info visit www.direct.gov.uk (see waste and recycling), www.communitycompost.org and www.lovefoodhatewaste.org.

5: Nappies

Cloth nappy questions

If you need practical advice about dealing with washables call the Real Nappy Helpline on 0845 850 0606, visit www.goreal.org.uk or check out www.thenappylady.co.uk, which offers home visits so you can match your baby's gender and drying arrangements with the best washable nappy.

Composting nappies

Compost worms are tricky to keep thriving if you aren't sensitive to their dislike of onions, citrus and a big pile of nappies, however biodegradable. One nappy, occasionally, will be enough for your tigers. Find more info about compost worm bins at www.wigglywigglers.com.

Eco chic areas

Places like Ballymena, Bath, Brighton, Bristol, Cheltenham, Hebden Bridge, Glastonbury, Hove, Leicester, Lewes, Llanidloes, Machynlleth, Monmouth, Oxford, Saltaire, Stroud, Totnes, Wivenhoe or London's Stoke Newington have reputations as being green areas. Find out if this is true by asking mums there, via internet forums or through friends, for useful tips about nappuccinos, recycling, baby activities etc.

Laundry service

Find out where your nearest nappy laundry service is by using the guide from the Real Nappy Information Service, see www.goreal.org.uk or ask your local council. Also try the UK Nappy Line at www.nappyline.co.uk and The National Association of Nappy Services at www.changeanappy.co.uk.

No nappies (elimination communication/EC)

Find out how to do it in Ingrid Bauer's *Diaper Free: The Gentle Wisdom of Natural Infant Hygiene* (Plume, 2008) a couple of months before your baby is born as it works most effectively if you give it an early start. Also see www.ehow.com, www.the ecstore.com and some of the YouTube shorts which show very young babies weeing when a hissing cue is made.

6: Time with Your Baby

Cyber friends for mums

You may only have chatted to your baby today so far, but you can share and enjoy childcare dreams, disasters and dilemmas using the net. Everyone seems to log on to www.mumsnet. com (and you can get a weekly round-up of mum gossip straight into your inbox). Also have a look at:

- Most recent Facebook sites (check the groups)
- Treehugger, an online community for green jobs, guides, etc., at www.treehugger.com
- *The Green Parent* magazine at www.greenparent.co.uk for articles, lots of discussion and the opportunity to track down other green mums on the meet-up page
- *Juno* magazine at www.junomagazine.com, which focuses on eco-conscious parenting
- Babycentre at www.babycentre.com
- Nappyvalley at www.nappyvalley.co.uk, an online market for selling nearly new items
- The NCT email list – or join a tea group of the National Childbirth Trust at www.nctpregnancyandbabycare.org.uk

Useful books

There are some very good natural remedy recipes in James Wong's *Grow Your Own Drugs* (Collins, 2009), or search the internet for precise instructions.

7: Sleeping, Baths and No-Fee Babysitting

Baths

Find out more about the hygiene hypothesis at www.hygien-ehypothesis.com.

For a fascinating book which charts the pregnancy of campaigner Sandra Steingraber's baby see *Having Faith: An Ecologist's Journey to Motherhood* (Berkley, 2001). It covers the issue of exposure to toxic chemicals both inside and outside the womb, and helps make it clear that it's not just the dose of poison that can be a problem to a foetus or child, it's the timing.

Sleep issues

Find lively debate and advice at www.babycentre.co.uk, chat at www.mumsnet.com and useful help at www.continuum-concept.org.

Books to read if you are interested in co-sleeping include *Three in a Bed: The Benefits of Sleeping with Your Baby* by Deborah Jackson (Bloomsbury, 2003). Also see the *Continuum Concept* by Jean Liedloff (Penguin, 2004).

For information on cot death, order the free leaflet *Reduce the Risk of Cot Death* from FSID (Foundation for the Study of Infant Deaths) at www.fsid.org.uk.

8: Getting Around

Buggies

Search the internet for 'buggy repairs' to find info on servicing, repairs and parts near you.

Find out where your nearest Maclaren dealer is at www.maclarenbaby.com. Their warranty doesn't cover fading covers, use with other children, second-hand purchases or the normal wearing down of wheels, but it is still an incentive to keep the receipt if you buy one.

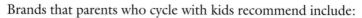

Cycling

Brands that parents who cycle with kids recommend include:

- The foldable Bike Friday Family Tandem, www.bikefold. com/bike_friday_family_tandem_traveler.htm
- Christiania, which is a load-carrying trike incredibly popular in Copenhagen. See www.christianiabikes.com/english/uk_main.htm
- Kangaroo, a Danish family bike for children from six months to 12 years, www.kangaroobike.com
- Nihola, a popular but rather expensive Danish model, http://.zerocouriers.com/workbike/zero/nihola.htm
- Onderwater models which fit two kids in front of the adult, see www.workcycles.com
- Triobike, which converts from a single bike or pushchair into a family bike with space for two children. See www.triobike.co.uk

To hire or buy specialist and unusual bikes in London see www.londonrecumbents.com. Their website includes information on lessons, trial sessions, bikes for special needs and bike parties.

Driving

To find out about ways to drive more fuel-efficiently, see the Energy Saving Trust's website www.energysavingtrust.or.uk/cars-travel-and-driving. You can also cut your fuel bill by studying the government's surprisingly useful page http://campaigns2.direct.gov.uk/actonco2/home/on-the-move.html. It includes good driving tips, a bar chart so you can compare the fuel costs and CO_2 emissions of all new cars, plus advice on sharing cars, etc. To make your travel miles less of a guessing game, See 'Journey CO_2' at www.transportdirect.info.

You can find your nearest car club at www.carclub.org.uk or share your journey by looking for a lift/or offering a ride at www.liftshare.com, www.nationalcarshare.co.uk and www.isany onegoingto.com.

Learn more about making streets safer for pedestrians at www.livingstreets.org.uk or other transport campaigning groups, such as www.bettertransport.org.uk.

Public transport

Find out how to get around at www.traveline.org.uk, or call 0871 200 22 33. You can find train timetables and information about railcards at www.nationalrail.co.uk, or call 0871 200 49 50. Local rail stations can also provide this info. Family railcards cut the cost of train travel, but if you want to book a seat for your toddler you will need a ticket, and sometimes this may be cheaper if you use a Groupsave ticket.

For family rail journeys out of the UK see www. seat61.com.

Slings

Brands that mums recommend include Ergo, Sasa Slings, Baby Bean, Big Mama Slings all available at UK Babywearing Swap, a yahoo group for buying and selling second-hand slings, or try eBay. You can also get good advice at www.slingmeet. co.uk. Also look at the Continuum Concept parenting forum at www.continuum-concept.org. A popular front-carrier brand is the Baby Bjorn.

9: Value Local Life

Get skilled up

The following organisations provide various courses around the country:

O British Trust for Conservation Volunteers, www.btcv. org.uk, which has its headquarters in Doncaster, runs workdays and courses to develop quintessentially British eco-system management (e.g., fencing, wildflower meadow management, care of tools).

O Low-Impact Living Initiative in Bucks, www.low impact.org, offers a wide range of courses, including solar hot water, woodland skills and cob building.

O The Centre for Alternative Technology, Machynlleth, Wales develops your DIY and energy-efficiency skills on its short courses. It's also a good place for a touristy day out – access it in a water powered lift. See www.cat.org.uk.

O The National Trust has recently run car tyre building, foraging and organic gardening courses. See www.national trust.org.uk.

O Neals Yard Remedies – the organic herbal apothecary – offers courses, remedies and recipes at www.nealsyard remedies.com.

O If you want something more thoughtful about adapting to a low-carbon society try Schumacher College, which specialises in tranformative learning for sustainable living. The college is near Totnes, Devon. Its 2009 courses focused on soul, ecosystems and thinking small. See www.schumachercollege.org.uk.

Look out for interesting courses in the press, at farm shops and the back of publications such as *Clean Slate, Resurgence*, www.theecologist.org and Friends of the Earth's supporter magazine, *Earthmatters*. Most of these courses require a fee, but there may be subsidies. Local newspapers and council free sheets often publicise dates and times of subsidised courses – not just dancing (although that's fun), but also the opportunity to learn green DIY; organic gardening; pruning fruit trees (did you know that the definition of a small orchard is a plot with just five trees?) or repairing/reshaping 'vintage' clothes.

Net friends to swap and try green ideas

Great places to network online include:

- www.treehugger.com
- http://sharonastyk.com
- http://myzerowaste.com
- www.thegreenparent.co.uk
- www.greenevents.co.uk
- www.greenbargainsblog.com
- www.naturalcollection.com
- www.ooffoo.com

School governors

Schools have million-pound budgets and a willingness to do things greener. Find out more about how to become a governor at www.direct.gov.uk.en/parents or visit www.sgoss.org.uk.

Volunteering

Two-fifths of volunteers said the opportunity to improve and learn new skills had prompted them to volunteer, with spoken communication skills (44%), team working (42%) and problem solving (39%) as the most sought-after outcomes. You can find out more about volunteering at www.timebank.org.uk.

There are 500,000 community organisations in the UK, many of these are helping their members become more environmentally sustainable. See www.everyactioncounts.org.uk.

Inspiring and easy to follow (mostly eco) suggestions can be found at We Are What We Do (the team behind *Change the World for a Fiver*). See www.wearewhatwedo.org.

Bibliography

Essential Reading

Jean Liedkoff, *The Continuum Concept* (Penguin, 2004)
Gabrielle Palmer, *The Politics of Breastfeeding* (3rd edition, Pinter and Martin, 2009)

Introduction: Bringing up Baby Green

Child Poverty Action Group, 'Child Wellbeing and Child poverty: Where the UK stands in the European table', 21 April 2009, www.cpag.org.uk/press/2009/210409.htm
Liverpool Victoria, 'The Cost of Raising a Child Tops £200,000', 23 February 2010, www.lv.com/media_centre/press_releases/lv-cost-of-a-child-survey-2010
The Optimum Population Trust, 'Contraception is "Greenest" Technology: Family planning cheapest way to combat climate change', 9 September 2009, www.optimumpopulation.org/releases/opt.release09Sep09
Andrew Simms, 'Planet Crunch', in *Resurgence*, No. 253, March/April 2009, pp.14–15

1: Give Your Home a Green Makeover

Friends of the Earth, 'Poisoning Our Children: The Dangers of Exposure to Untested and Toxic Chemicals,' September 1998, www.foe.co.uk/resource/briefings/poisoning_our_children.pdf

2: Shopping

Defra, 'Summary Report: Second sustainable clothing roadmap stakeholder meeting (March 2008)', May 2008, www.defra.gov.uk/environment/business/products/roadmaps/clothing/index.htm

3: Gift and Celebrations

'What to Do With Unwanted Christmas Gifts', *Telegraph*, 23 December 2007, www.telegraph.co.uk/finance/news bysector/retailandconsumer/2821635/What-to-do-with-unwanted-Christmas-gifts.html

Lucy Siegle, 'How Ethical are Children's Toys?', *Observer*, 2 December 2007, www.guardian.co.uk/lifeandstyle/2007/dec/02/ethicalliving

4: Food – What's Your Child Eating

Valerie Elliott, 'Cow&Gate and Farley's Rusks Attacked for Fat, Sugar and Salt Content', *The Times*, 4 May 2009, www.timesonline.co.uk/tol/news/uk/health/article 6216207.ece

Friends of the Earth, 'What's Feeding Our Food?', December 2008, www.foe.co.uk/resource/briefings/livestock_impacts_summary.pdf

Tim Hayward, 'Gordon Brown Makes a Hash of it: The prime minister has revealed his favourite dish – rumbledethumps', *The Times*, 5 January 2009, www.guardian. co.uk/lifeand style/wordofmouth/2009/jan/05/gordon-brown-favourite-food

Karen McVeigh, 'Vegetarians Less Likely to Develop Cancer Than Meat Eaters, says study', *Guardian*, 1 July 2009, www. guardian.co.uk/science/2009/jul/01/vegetarians-blood-cancer-diet-risk

NCT 'Position Statements and Journalism Briefings', www.nctpregnancyandbabycare.com/press–office/ position–statements

Michael Pollan, *In Defense of Food: An Eater's Manifesto* (Penguin, 2009)

'Organic milk is not healthier, says food watchdog', 21 September 2006, www.dailymail.co.uk/news/article-406155/Organic-milk-healthier-says-food-watchdog.html

Vegetarian Society, 'Why it's Green to go Vegetarian', Vegetarian Society website, 2009, www.vegsoc.org/ environment/why%20its%20green%20final%20small.pdf

World Health Organization and UNICEF, 'Global Strategy for Infant and Young Child Feeding', 2003, www.who.int/ nutrition/publications/infantfeeding/9241562218/ en/index.html

5: Nappies

Environment Agency, 'An updated lifecycle assessment study for disposable and reusable nappies (Science Report – SC010018/SR2)', October 2008, randd.defra.gov.uk/ Document.aspx?Document=WR0705_7589_FRP.pdf

Louise Gray, 'Nappies: Terry Cloth More Environmentally Friendly Than Disposable', 17 October 2008, www.telegraph. co.uk/earth/earthnews/3353497/Nappies-terry-cloth-more-environmentally-friendly-than-disposable.html

Five News, Nappy Debate, broadcast 21 May 2008

Women's Environmental Network, 'The "nappy" question!', 17 October 2008, www.lga.gov.uk/lga/aio/418961

8: Valuing Local Life

YouthNet, 'New report reveals benefits of volunteering', 2008, www.youthnet.org/YouthNet.org/MediaandCampaigns/ PressReleases/VolunteerSatisfactionSurvey

Index

jobs, rethinking 233–6

Kerr, Judith 86
kettle, filling 24

La Leche League 102, 254
labels, reading 177
laws, be empowered by new 226–7
learning with your baby 2, 6, 9–11,
229–30, 231, 263–4
libraries 10, 24, 52, 57, 73, 86, 91,
160, 176, 200, 224, 248 *see also*
toys
LILI (Low Impact Living
Initiative) 229–30, 263
limescale, lemons for 46
Little Guide to Trees, A (Voake) 82
Little Guide to Wild Flowers, A
(Voake) 82
local life, valuing 4, 10, 215–24,
231, 263–5
being active locally 222–4
case study 223–4
dreaming up changes 218–20
green 'values' 217–18
ideas for fundraising 220–1
neighbourhood, using your 9,
10, 73, 161, 216, 218, 219,
222, 226, 229, 231, 237, 252
London College of Fashion 68
London Recumbents 206

Marie Curie 65
Marine Stewardship Council
(MSC) 108, 109
maternity leave 10, 29, 104, 128,
149, 180, 230
McCartney, Stella 68
Maclaren buggy 197–8, 260
MDF 36
Mead, Margaret 216
mending 2, 6, 9, 46, 69, 197, 198,
214, 253
microwaves 43–4, 104

Mitchell, June Kumar 242
Mitchell, Mukti 242–3
Mitchell, Satish 242
mobile phones 44–5, 248
mobiles 9
monitor:
baby 1, 52, 172
energy 24, 49
Moses basket 53, 58, 170, 197
Murphy, Dominic 119
Myer, Andrew 15

Nadel, Jennifer 225–6
nails, cutting 9
nannies 4, 235
nappies 124–43, 147–8, 257–8
best and worst 133
bleach, using 144
case study 125
champion 148
changing mat 1, 54, 140, 142,
143, 147
cloth 1, 64, 126, 130, 134, 135,
136, 137, 138, 139, 257, 268
composting 125, 126, 128, 129,
133, 134, 147, 257
crises, solving 136–7
disposable 8, 124, 125, 126–9,
143
drying 138–9, 147
eco chic 257–8
elimination communication
(EC) 131–3, 148, 258
fabric conditioner 144
grants 131, 142, 147
how to change a nappy 139–41
laundry service 8, 125, 127,
131, 133, 134, 135, 138 142,
147, 258
liners, biodegradable 134
make your own washable 135
nappy bags 143–4
nappy networking 141–2
nappy-free playtime 148

Reading *see* books
recipes, for playing, fun 151–2
recycling 8, 63, 179, 207, 222,
  228, 238–9, 251, 253
  baby shower 57
  batteries 25
  clothes 71
  food waste 110, 121, 257
  gifts 84
  insulation and 19
  introducing children to idea of
    6, 11
  nappies 127, 130
  school 240
  shelves and 36
renewable energy 4, 21–2, 23, 24,
  25, 48, 245
renewable energy companies 4,
  21–2, 23, 25, 48
Resurgence 242
reusing items 3, 27, 36, 51, 59, 61,
  68, 130, 138, 157, 178, 213,
  235, 251 *see also* second-hand
room, baby's 29–31
  flooring 34–5
  heating 36–9
  lighting 35
  painting 31–3
  photo art 31
  safety 39–42
  sharing bed/bedroom 31
  shelves and storage 31, 35–6
  tips for keeping babies cool 37
  tips for keeping toddlers warm
    38
Rutherford, Jonathan 233–4

safety 249
  cupboards 39–40
  DIY materials 42
  falls 40–1
  injuries to baby 40–1
  plug sockets and air fresheners 41
  sharp corners 41–2

Teflon 42
Saltaire Village Society 220
Sandberg, Marlene 128
school:
  forest 163
  governors 10, 227, 264
  help your nearest 227
  private 3
  travelling to 199
scrap store, make a 153–4
scrapbook, make a 75
Scrapstore 33
seasons 154
second-hand 240, 260
  books 91, 176
  car seats 211
  cars 208, 209
  clothes 5, 56, 57, 64, 65–6, 70,
    84
  cots 171
  gifts 84, 85, 87, 88, 91
  insulation 19
  internet sites 12, 13
  Moses basket 170
  nappies 136
  shopping 50, 53, 54, 55–7,
    64–5, 70, 73, 159
  slings 191, 262
  toys 32
self-sufficiency 6, 119
sewing 73, 154
shampoo 178
shared memories 86–7
sharing the work 11–12
shopping 50–73, 250–2
  baby monitor 52
  books *see* books
  buggy *see* buggy
  certified products 250
  changing mat and nappy pack,
    easy-to-carry travel 54
  charity shops 10, 31, 32, 38, 42,
    51, 53, 56, 57, 58, 64, 65, 66,
    67, 69, 73, 90, 200